Rooted in Faith

Farangiss Sedaghatpour

Rooted in Faith

Copyright © 2021 by Farangiss Sedaghatpour

All rights reserved. No part of this book may be reproduced or transmitted in any form or by any means without written permission of the author.

ISBN 978-1-7321172-2-8

Acknowlegments

Thank you to my dear parents, Rashel and Jamshid Shaye, for their love and support at all times.

Thank you to my children, Sean, Devorah, Dillon, and Dinah Sedaghatpour, for being the apple of my eyes.

Thank you to my grandchildren, Leah Sarah, Meir Aaron, Shimon, for being my heart.

Thank you to all my aunts, uncles, cousins, for their continuous love.

Last but not least, thank you to all my friends, who make space for me in their lives, and give me the gift of their time, and connection.

Thank you to Farnaz Delafraz for painting front and back cover.

Thank you to Shahram Delafraz for patiently writing all the words on the tree branches of the painting.

Your love and kindness emanates through them.

My gratitude, to my Rebbe, The Nikolsburg Rebbe, for being the light in my times of darkness, a force of goodness and compassion, and the voice of Divinity.

Thank you to Rabbi Polikoff, Rabbi Lichter, and all Great Neck Synagogue members for embracing my family and I.

I am who I am because of all of you.

Thank you!

Introduction

It's not in the norm of my everyday life, that I'm pushed to create something and almost with urgency.

It was a Thursday morning, February 13th 2020, as I was looking out through my dining room window at the snow sitting on the trees, and making beautiful landscape of white, and shimmering ice in the sun, I was moved to create a WhatsApp group, and called it, "Rooted in Emuna", Emuna being Hebrew for Faith. Over the next couple of days, Over 200 people had joined the group.

Little did I know then, that the group would carry us through the pandemic of our life-time, through crisis that evolved as a result of COVID, the loneliness the took over many of us, and the need for connection that was prevalent at the time.

I originally wanted to do 91 days of messaging, 91, being the numerical value of a righteous person in Hebrew. I had in mind my late husband, Vahid Sedaghatpour, whom in my mind I had dedicated it to.

After the 91 days, and stopping the messaging, there was still a need to continue, and so the format changed, from statements, to questions, and from questions, to words.

So much was evoked through these daily messages, which frankly I can't take any credit for, as I'm of the belief that the energy of the collective group was being channeled into these messages. It is what we needed at the time to uplift us, elevate us, even if for a moment.

Every morning at 7 am these messages would go out. There were people on this WhatsApp from Israel, Spain, California, Washington, Texas, and other states in US. It connected us.

The greatest gift of all…connection.

This book is a culmination of all the messages that was shared during that time, starting Feb 14th 2020, right before COVID, going all the way to May 16th of 2021, with some stops in between.

It has been an honor to have been part of this group.

I have changed the original name, "Rooted in Emuna", to "Rooted in Faith", so that if need be, it can reach more people across religions and continents.

These messages are universal.

Whatever walk of life we are from, whatever traditions we have, wherever we are born, Truths are Truths, that is Divine Truth is Divine Truth.

May all those who find themselves reaching out for this book, be elevated, by the group energies that is contained within this book.

Dedication

This book is dedicated to "Rooted in Emuna" WhatsApp group. Everyone collectively has a share in this book. Your energies are in these words, in the messages shared, in the writings, and in the connections that was created.

Thank you!

-1

To have faith doesn't only mean that we have faith in G-d that he will come through for us, protect us, guide us, and through Divine providence lead us to our highest destiny, but also that Creator of this entire universe who has created the galaxies & heavens, has faith in you, that YOU and only YOU are equipped with the spiritual DNA to beautify the space within and around you. G-d has faith in you that as his soldier on earth you do his bidding and sees with his infinite mind that you bring it to fruition.

If he didn't have faith in us, why else would we be here?

-2

The evolution of human consciousness is to go from a state of self-limiting contained consciousness, to a state of limitless Divine consciousness where it is ever flowing with the undercurrent of love, possibilities, & unified field of Divine oneness.

However, we are not to give up the self for the Divine but rather use the self to bring the Divine into the reality that we find ourselves in. We are to infuse our everyday reality, our personalities, our seemingly mundane goings and comings, our challenges and our successes with Divine Consciousness, understanding that each one of us is a fragment of the whole.

G-d has imbued us with the capacity of bridging the limited with limitless, of finite with infinite, of mundane with holy.

From beginning of time, there is a voice that's echoed every day that says, "where are you?" More precisely where are you on your path of conscious evolution? How are you participating in this and if not now then when?

-3

*W*hat does being strong mean?

We declare Chazak, chazak, Venitchazek, Be strong, be strong and you shall be strengthened, when finishing each book of Torah.

What are we exactly evoking when we say those words?

First, we must be cognizant of not equating strength with absence of pain, tears and sadness. There are times in one's life that it's what's so at the given moment. We must honor our humanity in face of a sad, and tragic event, or a very challenging situation that we might be faced with.

There are so many of us that when faced with a heart breaking situation, are afraid of tears or afraid to say they are in pain, for they feel that it's a lack of faith.

On the contrary, if we don't voice, if we don't cry, we haven't honored our humanity, and we aren't giving the situation compassion.

Second, the strength that G-d is asking of us, is the strength of connection.

G-d says:

"Be connected, be connected, and I make your connection even deeper and stronger, and from there you have to ability to rise up"

To have strength, is not only to have connection to G-d, the wellspring of healing & life, but also to become connected on a deeper level to one's soul, so that one is able to access the power that lies dormant within.

When we do that, we have the courage and fortitude to step forth in our lives with whatever situation and challenge we are handed with.

Strength then is no longer the measure of how well you withstand challenges, rather, it's a measure of how deeply you connect when challenges arise.

Reflect on this:

I am strong and courageous when I am connected. I walk forward with fortitude and knowingness as I am strengthened by G-d's light.

−4

The second of Ten Commandments, states that we shall not recognize G-d's of others in G-d's presence. This is a commandment against idol worship. Idol worship is defined not only as idols to bow to, or worship, but anything that's given power and dominion over G-d's power and will.

Idol worship in 20th century disguises itself in many different shapes and forms. It masks itself as the worship of status, power, & money. Not to say that status, power or money are bad, on the contrary they are great tools to work with. It only becomes idol worship when it's no longer used as a tool but an end unto itself. It's idol worship when it's dominion proceeds G-d's dominion, and when it's power is the only power.

Apart from these three, there is one idol worship that most of us fall prey to, and we must muster strength to eradicate it from our psyche. That is worry. Yes, to worry is to idol worship. We can be concerned, we can strategize, we can plan, and then we must release. To worry, is to say, there is the unknown and so many forces that can affect the outcome, and somehow I need to control the situation, rather than doing what we can in our best ability with everything we have, and then release it to G-d, having full trust that the outcome will be good, whatever it is.

Do you worry?

If yes, what about?

Can you do what you can for the situation, to your best ability and then Trust G-d that the rest is taken care of?

Are you willing to give up this form of subtle and yet exhausting idol worshipping?

-5

*C*hange is inevitable.
The natural order of life is movement, and with movement comes change.

If we look at the monthly cycles of the moon, we see that the moon waxes and wanes, coming to its fullness in the middle of its cycle. However, you can't hold the fullness in a static state, since the next day it wanes.

We see change in seasons, in the movement of the waves of ocean, no two wave being the same, in planetary cycles, in movement of river or stream.

So too with us, we are always changing, waxing and waning, from moment of birth. Sometimes we like the change, sometimes we don't. Some changes are elevating for us, and some changes heartbreaking.

The only common denominator in all of the changes in one's life is one thing and one thing only, our soul.

We have the same light when born, as when in our eighties, hopefully over course of time some of the light has been actualized.

Your body changes, goes from baby to adulthood, to middle age and then old age. However, your soul always has light, always has potential, always has what you need to go from one change to another, always has inherent power, and inherent wisdom.

H-Shem then relies on your soul, which is a constant in all of it, to carry it over, to utilize its powers to move from one change to another. H-Shem relies on the light of your soul to illuminate the path. He relies on your perseverance to step into the change. He relies on you to shift into the changed paradigm with great tenacity.

You might ask so what I shift or persevere or illuminate?

So that you are able to bring G-Dliness into all changes, be it a place of darkness or be it a place of light.

So that you become the Master over change, rather than change becoming the Master over you.

In that G-dliness, is a transformation that not even the greatest of angels are capable of.

-6

In the image of G-d man has been created.
What image might that be?

G-d's image is no image at all, He is The infinite, The possibility of possibilities, The No-thing, The undefinable, The unknowable.

We have been made in that image, the image of no image at all.

Our task then becomes breaking images of oneself continuously so we are able to resemble our creator as it has been intended.

We have an image about our personalities, our emotional makeup, of what's possible and what's not. We are to break that and enter into a realm of possibilities.

If we think, this is who I am, this is my emotional or mental makeup, then we have made an image.

If we think this is where I am in life, and I will never get out of this, then we have made an image.

Do you have an image of yourself?

It's your job, through freedom of choice that G-d has given you, to break the image, especially if it's unfavorable, and replace it with possibilities.

Do you have an image of your situation?

Your soul can never be defined or be kept in a prism of self. Unleash it by un-defining your circumstances, & situations.

Do not allow for anything or anyone to define you and be put you in a box. Do not allow for labels to define you and put you in a limitation.

Yes, you are let's say a Doctor, but you are not only that, you are much more than that, or a lawyer, or a mom or a dad.

You are much more than any of these.

To define yourself, is to limit yourself, and to limit what can be possible for you.

G-d in the very beginning of Torah gives us the secret to continuously grow, to become, to evolve, & to elevate.

The secret being:

In the image of G-d man has been created.

-7

The Thirteen Divine attributes of Mercy, are the attributes of G-d that was gifted to Moshe to be transmitted to all generations to come.

G-d has no image, however, he has attributes that express themselves in the physical world in various ways.

These thirteen attributes of Mercy, are the attributes of compassion, forgiveness, tremendous love, and connection.

In order to deepen our bond with our creator, we are to resemble him.

If G-d has no image that we can resemble, then how can we deepen that connection?

We are to resemble his attributes, specifically the thirteen Divine attributes of Mercy.

The ground work for attributes of Mercy is forgiveness.

Forgiveness is an essential ingredient in Judaism, since it binds us to a past, an event, a circumstance that no longer is present, however, through not forgiving it's carried over into present over and over and over again.

To start deepening our bond with G-d, and resembling his attributes of compassion, we need to start by looking at where do I need to grant forgiveness and to whom.

Forgiveness of past events, of the way life has presented itself, the way certain people have showed up or not, circumstance that have been painful, & people that have been hurtful.

Sometimes, the greatest forgiveness needs to be granted to self, for the way we have showed up with doubt, reservation about life and shyness to move forward, and everything else that gets in the way of living our highest self.

Where to begin?

Begin by looking at yesterday, does anything or anyone needs to be granted forgiveness?

Go back a week, then a year, then go back as long as you can, and loosen the rope of bondage.

If we are to break our images continuously in order to grow and to become, then forgiveness is just a natural process of that growth.

To forgive is the beginning of stepping into paradigm of compassion and love.

In this paradigm we resemble our creator and we become a reflection of Divine in the physical world.

-8

*T*he reality of illusion

There are so many on the path of mindfulness who struggle with what's real and what's illusion, and in that struggle try to adapt and adjust way of thinking according to the answers they come up with.

In Jewish thought, everything is real, every experience is real. Physicality is as real as spirituality, after all G-d has created it all, for G-d there is no separation. The world of physical is only contraction, and continuum of world of spiritual. We declare twice a day Shema Israel H-Shem Elokinu H-Shem Echad.

Echad is oneness of G-d in everything, in all levels of creation and all levels of being.

We are not to abandon the physical world for world of spirit, nor are we to abandon the spiritual world for physical reality. We are not to choose one world over the other. We are however, to infuse the two worlds together, we are to merge the two distinct realities together.

This is our ultimate accomplishment, to bring G-dliness into all aspects of physical existence.

If we say an experience, challenge, or hardship, is illusion, then how can we ever change the condition or transform it?

How can we ever find a solution to our problems, if we perceive the problems as illusions?

How can we be participants in Tikun Olam if pain doesn't exist?

No pain is an illusion.

No challenge is an illusion.

No circumstance is an illusion.

The same goes for the opposite.

No joy is an illusion.

No abundance is an illusion.

They might be transient and temporary but for the moment and time the person finds themselves in, it's very real.

Everything is real, and because everything is real, everything can be transformed.

Because everything is real, everything can be elevated to a level where G-Dliness can be breathed into.

And who can do this? Who is equipped with bringing G-dliness into any challenge, situation, and circumstance?

YOU and YOU only, because you possess both worlds, the physical and the spiritual.

If everything is real, then what's the illusion?

Illusion is to think that you are in it alone.

Illusion is to not know that G-d is holding your hand and hovering over you every step of the way.

Illusion is to think that your situation or condition will always stay the same and you will never get out of it.

Illusion is to think you don't have the strength, the man power, the knowhow of getting through the situation.

Illusion is to think you are stuck.

Illusion is to not know that you are guided and G-d sends his angels to guide you on your path.

Illusion is to have forgotten about your soul that has all the power, all the knowing, all the light, and the direct connection to G-d to bring you the solutions that you need at hand at that very moment.

The reality of illusion is to not recognize yourself, the physical and spiritual self, and not to take the opportunity to elevate all that is around you at the present moment, where ever you find yourself at.

−9

*W*hat is your worth?

If you were to answer the question without reading on, how would you answer this question?

Please take a moment to contemplate and answer. Don't change your answer, just what comes naturally.

How do you gauge this worth?

What is it based on?

What are the parameters for this worth?

We gauge our worth in relation to others, circumstance, status, and what we have accomplished or not. It's always in relation to……, and according to that we make an evaluation.

Our worth however, is NOT to be gauged, it's NOT to be valued in relation to…..

In reality our worth is always a constant as in relation with G-d. We are always worthy of his love, his guidance, his protection, his benevolence.

Our worth is just what's so by the mere fact that we are here in this moment, living, breathing and being, and G-d has made us his co-pilot in this world to bring G-dliness, goodness, love, compassion, in our corner of the world, in every second that we are here.

We have inherent worth that is not effected by standards of society, circumstances, nor by the accomplishments made.

Why is it important to be rooted in that inherent worth?

Unless you see yourself worthy, you will not step forth with fortitude into the new moment and bring your gifts and talents into this physical reality to be used to beautify this world.

Being grounded in your inherent worth also brings great humility.

Worth and humility sound like two opposites, yet they feed each other and are effected by each other.

Moshe Rabbeinu was the humblest of all man for all times to come. If he had shied away from his connection to H-Shem, and from his gifts—which he did in the beginning—he could have never been the channel for all that prophecy, teaching, transmission of Ten Commandments and Torah. He was extremely humble, yet he had inherent worth that he be the light that he came to be, the channel for H-shem's love for us in its fullest expression.

Your inherent worth gives you permission, with great humility, to be the force and the light that you came to be.

Now answer the question:

What is your worth?

-10

The joyous month—Adar

Month of Adar is of the characteristic that asks of us to increase in joy day after day.

How can one increase in joy tomorrow knowing that most probably the circumstances, situations, condition of today carry over to tomorrow and throughout the month.

Are we to pretend that I'm happier today than yesterday and I'll be happier tomorrow than today?

We are not to pretend, rather we are to connect to the energy, every day a bit more than the day before.

The best metaphor for this would be:

Imagine it's raining, and you are assigned to collect rain water that's needed for places that doesn't have rain and also for a time in future.

The amount of rain collected is equivalent to the size of your container. Your container could be a cup, a jar, large bowl, large pot or it could even be a swimming pool size container.

The rain is coming, it's up to you how much you collect.

In this metaphor, rain is joy and container is consciousness.

The joy is to be tapped into, how much you tap into, depends entirely on your consciousness.

We are asked to be mindful of our containers, we are to become a bit more conscious as each day comes to pass.

When becoming conscious, it's not to say that the surrounding is changing, although joy absolutely shifts your surroundings, it's to say that every day I'm expanding the way I'm experiencing my life. I'm choosing gratitude over complaining, I'm choosing to see my life from a place of blessings rather than otherwise. I'm choosing to see the good in everything, every event, and everyone, I'm choosing to be alive with joy of just being.

Joy is not the end unto itself but rather a vehicle to break through all barriers.

Barriers come in many shapes and forms. Barriers from within, barriers of connecting to other, barriers of connecting to yourself, barriers of connecting to H-Shem, barriers of being limited, barriers of fully being in this world.

Joy breaks through all barriers.

In that breaking through, shifts happen, and in that miracles happen.

Give yourself this gift of joy this month.

Don't shy away from it because your circumstances might dictate otherwise.

Be the greatest act of courage....to be in joy regardless.

This my dear friend is faith in action.

-11

The tenth commandment states that we should not covet someone else's belongings.

This is a commandment against a certain way of thinking. It's asking us to not look at what someone else possesses and then want it for ourselves.

Can you imagine, the Ten Commandments being given to Jewish people in all of its glory and it's concerned about how I'm seeing/thinking about my neighbor, friend, associate?

And why is coveting the 10th commandment?

The 10th commandment encompasses all the other commandments, to the extent that if we are not aligned with the 10th commandment, there is a part of us that's not aligned with all other 9.

If we covet something that someone else has, at the core of it means,

1. We are not trusting G-d that I am exactly where I need to be.

2. We are not acknowledging the gifts and blessings that G-d has given us.
3. We are falling short of being grateful.
4. We are not trusting ourselves.
5. We might go to any length to obtain that very thing that someone else has to our own detriment.
6. We become needy, greedy, and distasteful.
7. Our lives become a comparison mode.

The worst thing we can do to ourselves is to compare our lives with others. By comparing we diminish who we are and where we are at.

To compare is to covet, which is a prohibition.

We must become mindful of something that's so prevalent, to compare ourselves-our status, & our belongings with others, for that's the infestation of mind and emotion that can affect all the other 9 commandments.

The remedy,

Be grateful for all that you have.

Be appreciative for all that has presented itself.

Trust G-d that he brings you all your resources. Move forward in joy and with joy.

-12

The teachings of Corona virus:

1. We all have an impact on each other.

It's easy to think of ourselves as separate entities that won't have much an impact on the whole.

In Judaism, every thought, speech and action can have an impact on the whole humanity, to an extent that it has the potential of changing its destiny.

Corona virus shows us how interconnected & intertwined we all are.

2. It's not the smallness of something

But rather the potency of something.

Never underestimate the smallest act of kindness. Never underestimate its potency, for you have no idea how one smile, one hug, one compliment, can impact the person.

Corona virus is tiny and yet it's potent in wrecking havoc.

3. The gift of being solution oriented.

Yes, corona virus has induced much fear globally. However, it doesn't help anyone to be frozen in fear. If frozen in fear, everything becomes magnified 10 fold.

We learn that when situations arise, even situations that are extraordinary, painful and shocking, we must become solution oriented, we can't afford to stay in fear and panic, but rather what can I do today? What's required of me today?

4. The gift of collaboration.

Solutions are made much faster and more efficiently when we are together.

It's a gift to be together, to have each other, whether it shows up as family or friends or both.

5. If there are no solutions in sight, don't loose hope, keep going at it, and have faith that solutions are there waiting to be found.

There are no solutions to Corona virus, but the entire scientific community is working on making a vaccine.

How can we combat corona virus spiritually?

Learn from it and the do exactly that.

Know with 100% certainty that you effect the whole.

Know with 100% certainty that we are all connected.

Know with 100% certainty one act of kindness can change the destiny of whole world no matter how small.

Change fear of a situation to faith, knowing that solution is waiting to be discovered.

Know that together solutions that would seem impossible become possible.

Now, go out there and do random acts of kindness. It's contagious and its potent.

Let's create healing for each other by the smallest act of goodness.

May our smallest act of kindness be a catalyst for the healing of all.

Note: please don't take these words as meaning that you shouldn't take good practice in prevention, washing hands regularly, keeping body hydrated, & keeping immune system strong, keeping in mind that fear actually decreases the immune system.

-13

G-d as our bestie:

We have many different relationships with G-d, G-d as our king, G-d as our parent, G-d as our beloved, and of course G-d as our creator.

He is always all of it to us, however, the manifestation of the relationship differs according to the time of the year.

In Rosh Hoshana We relate to him as our king & creator.

In Passover We relate to Him our love.

In Tisha B'av We relate to Him as our father.

How about our every day in and day outs of life? How about the mundane, non-eventful times of life? How about the challenging painful times of our lives?

G-d has the greatest desire that He becomes our bestie, that He becomes our best friend, the one whom we confide in, the one who won't judge me for how I'm feeling, my failures, my weaknesses.

The one who knows my humanity, and knows my deepest fears, my deepest strengths, my knowing, and desires.

The one who can hold a space to be, pour love into the situation, and hold me in his embrace.

G-d desires us to share with him everything, even though He is aware of all of it. He desires to be present in every aspect of our lives. He desires to hold our hands through it all, and be the source of power in our lives. He desires to be present and share our joys and pains, our triumphs and failures, our moments of inspiration and moments of despair.

The greatest pain-metaphorically speaking-for G-d is, for us to deny him of that relationship, and to deny him of giving his unconditional love and attention to us.

There is one requirement from us, to extend our hands so G-d can hold our hand, so He can walk with us through the journey of our lives.

Next time you need a friend, extend your hand to G-d by telling him what's on your mind, how you are feeling, what you are looking for, and then wait for the answers to come through, wait for the light to shine through, wait for the inspiration to flow through.

Most of us are afraid of an intimate relationship with G-d because we feel our closeness will make us be seen more clearly and our shortcomings will be enhanced in eyes of G-d. On the contrary, it's our distance with Him, that enhances our shortcomings, since we have distanced ourselves from his love and power.

We might think that the reward of such a relationship is that I will start seeing miracles in my life, because I have such a close relationship with G-d. This is absolutely true but the greatest reward is the relationship itself, the closeness, the embrace, the feeling of safety, the strength and the love.

In this time of the year that we are supposed to connect to joy, let us also bring the greatest joy to G-d, to extend our hands to Him so he can hold our hands, and let Him know that we desire for Him to be our best friend, as well as King, Father, & Beloved.

-14

Principles of speech:

Are the words that are coming out of my mouth compassionate?

Are the words that are coming out of my mouth helpful?

Are the words that are coming out of my mouth creating a space of safety for other to share?

The answer to all the above should be "yes" before starting a conversation.

Mastery of self begins by mastering the WAY we have conversations.

—15

Listening as a form of compassion

Compassion is when one is able to hold a space for the other to be their truest self in the moment, while pouring in love for them, so they can better move through whatever pain or situation they are in.

Listening to a person tell their story, their pain, their heartbreak, is one of the greatest act of compassion.

In Judaism we say Shema Israel twice a day.

Shema means to hear, to listen.

It doesn't say "see Israel", it doesn't say "think Israel", it doesn't say "be aware Israel", it says "listen Israel"

We are a nation of listeners. Our connection to spirituality and G-d starts by listening.

Becoming more compassionate, means first you have to become a better listener.

Practice this today:

Allow someone to tell their story, to relay how they are feeling, what's causing them pain,

1. without putting yourself into the equation. So many times when someone is sharing their pain, we have the habit of jumping right in and saying oh this happened to me too.

2. Please never compare someone's pain with yourself or someone else. Please never say well, mine is worse or someone else is worse, what would you do if you were so and so.

3. Don't spiritualize someone's pain. That's inhumane. You can only spiritualize your own pain.

4. Don't put your own logic into someone's challenging situation. This happened to you so this and that happens..

5. Allow them to be heard, support them by being a voice of care, love, & warmth.

For today just listen and practice the art of compassion.

-16

Moshe Rabbeinu Birthday & Yartzeit (date of passing)

The birth of Moshe Rabbeinu has given the Jewish people for all time, the strength and light to be a miraculous nation.

He was the channel and G-d's partner in manifesting all the miracles, both in Egypt and in dessert. Through him the Ten Commandments and all of Torah was transmitted.

He remains that channel for miracles to continue manifesting, however, he needs every single one of us to manifest G-d's light into physical reality.

Moshe, our teacher, and prophet needs every single one of us to be on board with him, to bring a revelation that started some 3,000 years ago into fruition.

You ask, and how do I do that?

You do that by connecting to a light that's beyond you and yet is within you.

You do that with unshakable faith that my greatest contribution to this earth and to this life is when I can stand humbly and yet with confidence, to infuse goodness, light, and strength in the small part of the world that I find myself in.

In that space, you are exactly where you need to be in order-to be the channel for G-d's light and for miracles to manifest.

-17

*W*e all have capacity of choice
We all have capacity of change

There are many universal laws at work at all times, one of them being the laws of cause and effect.

These universal laws apply on a physical level and energetic level.

It's a law and works whether we are conscious of it or not.

Every time we think, speak, and act we are creating an energy or at best shifting the energy to a certain direction.

Thoughts of joy, unity, love, seeing the good in all things, and people, seeing the spark of good in everything, trust, & faith, lightens the world and loosens the hold of negativity.

Negativity could be anything, fear, challenges that show up in many different shapes and forms, & diseases.

We have the capacity to shift the scale, to balance the energetic profile, and to make things move in direction of goodness and light.

With our everyday choices, we make changes.

Know that every choice on any level, has the capacity of shifting mountains.

Also know that it's not up to us to decide which choice is small and which is large.

We will also never know the full impact of our daily choices.

Practice this:

Be mindful of your choices for today.

If you say or do something out of habit, think again, you have the capacity of choice and you have the capacity to change, and shift the energy and ultimately world around you.

Shift one thought.

Shift one spoken sentence.

Shift one action.

-18

*O*ne must be able to define success in-order to move towards it.

Success of a human being in the grand scheme of the universe is not measured by the daily so called failures, up and downs, wins and losses, but rather by the meaning, purpose, connection, & direction we give our lives.

If we define our lives as some random act of nature, then everything we do or don't do is based on that randomness, and everything that happens is haphazard, just some force of nature, which we call bad luck, or good luck.

If, however, we define our lives as purposeful, meaningful, and participants in directing the world into its fullest destiny, then everything we do and say is directed towards that meaning and purpose. In this space there are no random acts of nature, nothing is haphazard, and no situation is based on luck.

Success then is the ability to direct and redirect our lives towards a life of purpose, to be able to take out of equation the idea of good luck and bad luck, for that gives the power of our lives to some random idea called luck. To be able to steer our lives toward a life of connection, and align ourselves to a life of meaning that's for the highest good of all.

-19

*W*hat does love encompass?
Love in its truest sense is, I SEE YOU.

I see you beyond your physical appearance.

I see you beyond your challenges, pain and circumstances.

I see you in your joy and I see you in your pain.

I see you in the light that you are.

I see you in your greatest potential.

I see you with all your goodness, knowing that at this moment not all of your goodness is even apparent to yourself.

I see you as all you can be, knowing that at this moment, you think of yourself as a fraction of all that you are.

I see your strength, your will, your courage, knowing that at this moment you are experiencing yourself as not so.

You are fully known to me, and in that knowing I invite you to see yourself as I see you, all of you.

In Judaism we are commanded to love our neighbor as we love ourselves. It means that we must train ourselves to see beyond their circumstances, and appearances, and see them in the light that they are. We must train ourselves to have a sight that sees the potential, the goodness that they inherently have, giving them the ability to rise beyond their own limitations.

It is through this love that we can become more than we are, no matter where we find ourselves at.

This training starts with self.

I see you, I know you, I love you.

-20

*T*he antithesis to joy is doubt

We are of the belief that our joy is lessened or increased by circumstances, outside forces, and people's presence and the way the show up or not.

Purim teaches us that joy is an internal well, a never ending supply of joy is available to us if we wish to regardless of anything outside of ourselves.

The one thing that stops the flow of this joy is doubt.

Doubt presents itself in many shapes and forms.

Doubt as fear

Doubt as worry

Doubt G-d's Dominance

Doubt G-d's involvement in every detail of our lives

Doubt G-d's healing power

Doubt G-d's love

When we doubt G-d we are also doubting ourselves.

Doubt the power that exists within

Doubt the knowingness of our soul

Doubt the light of our soul

Doubt our purpose

Doubt our existence and importance

On Purim we are asked to eradicate Amalek, which is same numerical value as doubt.

The most joyous day of the year, and we are asked to eradicate doubt.

Doubt creates uncertainty, despondency, inability to move forth, inability to make decisions, inability to have courage, inability to believe, and the question "what if I fail", "what if....."

Let the joy flow from your inner knowing and allow your feet to walk with faith. In this state of flow, you have privy to a state of self that's beyond the self, beyond the circumstances, problems and situations.

In this state, you are one with your soul and H-Shem.

In this state you have eradicated doubt and drinking from well of your joy.

-21

*E*very event matters in the unfolding of our lives

As human beings we like to categorize things into boxes of identification.

We even do this with events of our lives, categorizing some events as good, bad, happy, sad, etc. By doing that we like to forget some points or events of our lives while magnifying others.

Today we read Megilat Esther. The rule is to hear the whole Megillah being read, and not miss any part of it.

Why?

Because all the events that lead to the point of redemption matter. What we are reading is a 12 year story unfolding, and every single detail of it matters.

We might think one event matters over other, but no, all of it matters.

The same is true of our lives. Everything leads us to be where we are today, and what we do today will effect our future.

All of it matters. Our history and our story matters. The ups and downs that we have traveled, the people we have met on the way, the faith, strength, and resilience that we have built as we are moving through life, the tears we have shed, the laughters we have shared, the moments of loneliness and moments of great connection, all of it matters.

As our lives unfold, we must know that our history and individual story is precious, not leaving behind any part of it.

We must also know that we are active participants in this unfolding, and our choices of unity, kindness, can tip the scale towards light and joy, just like the choices Esther and Mordechai.

-22

*W*e reside in different levels of consciousness at the same time

The human being is the marvel of G-d's creation. We have many dynamics at play at the same time, emotions, the voice in our heads, the voice of our souls, our intuition, and the under current that's unknown to our conscious.

To bring all of these dynamics into harmony takes effort, reflection, introspection and a desire to navigate the different energies with knowledge.

This diversity in self is necessary in-order to reach, connect and hopefully transform different aspects of reality.

Having emotions is great, because it can add passion, love, and enthusiasm.

Having thoughts gives us the ability to reflect and steer accordingly.

There are schools of thought that say go with your heart, shut off the brain, the brain is too logical and judgemental.

Then there are schools of thought that say go with your brain, the heart is too emotional, whimsy, unpredictable.

Then comes Judaism and says use both, for everything is part of Divine design.

Connect your knowledge with love of your heart and then see how far you go.

Steer your thoughts with enthusiasm and see how you transform.

Guide your awareness with passion and see how you grow.

We are never to deny an aspect of ourselves, but rather to utilize everything we have been gifted with.

The goal is to reach a space where the voice of our soul guides our thought and redirect our emotions, weaving all aspects of self together.

23

Being a match lighter

Imagine you are outside and the weather is cold, it's dark. It's you and a few other people in middle of no where, trying to figure how to warm yourselves, and also warm others.

The first person says I have a jacket and sweater, I'll share with you, we can huddle together. You can get some warmth but it's still dark.

The second person says I have extra blankets that I can share with you. Again, you can get some warmth but it's still dark.

The third person says, I have a match, and with the match we will put on a fire. This way we have warmth and light.

Be a match lighter in times when it's dark and cold. Dark and cold represents times in our lives when we feel afraid, disconnected, challenged.

Be a match lighter, and light not only your space but space of others.

How to be a match lighter?

1st you need to light your own match, you need to light up your own self.

2nd you be a match lighter for others by being a source of stability, strength, hope, and most importantly taking a stance of faith and Trust.

For today, be a match lighter.

-24

*Y*our talents don't belong to you, but to the world, so stop making excuses.

The sun doesn't shine for its own sake, but for the world it illuminates and life that becomes possible because of it.

The moon has no light that it's even aware of. It just reflects light to illuminate the dark skies.

We have so many voices that stop us from fully stepping into our talents, which is a gift from G-d given to us to lighten our part of the world which we stand on.

The voice of "what will they say"

The voice of "who am I to even want to do this"

The voice of "it won't work"

All these voices are irrelevant. What's relevant is to engage that talent into this world so G-d can pour his creativity through you.

-25

*E*xtraordinary times require special attention.

We can't deny the fact that we are living in an extraordinary time.

We are always in communication with the world around us, the universe at large and G-d.

However, times like this we need to ask,

What is being communicated to us through all these events?

These are purely my thoughts:

Times like these requires introspection, reflection and reorientation.

We have all been put in a place of simplicity, going back to basics.

In this space of simplicity, it beckons the question,

what's important to me?

What's important in my life?

What's important for my family?

How do I bear responsibility for myself and others?

We must answer these questions, for the answers are the springboard to our growth, connection and reorientation.

Change one degree and you change the course of your ship and it's destination.

This extra-ordinary time gives us the opportunity for extra-ordinary growth.

To waste this incredible opportunity, is to have wasted all the fear and pain that we are going through as a community.

You, I, us, together can steer the ship of our collective destiny to a more elevated direction by choosing to do one thing that connects us more than we did yesterday.

One thing, and we have changed the collective destiny.

In this way, in our simplicity, we have also become extraordinary.

Maybe just maybe in all of this mayhem that's what's being communicated, be simple and humble, yet elevated, connected and extraordinary.

-26

Noach was ordered by G-d to enter the Arc, as the rain had started falling and it was the beginning of a 40 day saga, the flood.

Our sages tell us that the numerical dimensions of the arc mentioned in Torah, when changed to letters, it equals Lashon, tongue.

G-d is therefore ordering Noach not only to enter the Arc but enter the tongue or word.

A lesson for all generations as we are faced with floods of our times. Floods signifying a time of great challenge.

The arc of Noach also had a window or some sages say a stone called Tzohar, where in brightened the arc, and was a source of illumination.

Right here are the ingredients of entering into a space of safety and light as the floods are surging around us.

The secret is our words.

With our words we create. There is no doubt about it that words have a creative power. We must become conscious of how we are using this creative power and use it to not only be an Arc for us, where we are safe, but also in our safety we are illuminated.

The words are words of

Gratitude

Prayer

Positivity

Encouragement

Hope

Saying only good about others or at best,

Refraining from using bad words

Refraining from slander

Refraining from putting others down

Refraining from putting ourself down

Words of illumination,

Faith

Trust

Words of connection

Love

Compassion

Hearing each other out

Noach was ordered to enter the Arc.

We are ordered to enter the word.

Let our words be a source of protection and illumination for us, our families and our communities at this time of calamity and challenge.

Use your words wisely and unleash its creative power.

-27

*O*ur humanity dictates that we have ups and downs, that we oscillate with different emotions, that we have contradictory thoughts all in one day.

Our humanity is designed for survival and anything that threatens that survival brings out intense emotions, namely fear and extended fear which we call panic.

Fear and panic is felt in one's psyche when we feel out of control, when our norm is shaken up, when the ground we stand on feels unstable and everything normal has been put into a question mark.

We are not to deny our humanity, however, it is possible to transcend our humanity if we choose to.

First and foremost we are gifted with freedom of choice. It seems many choices are stripped from us these day, but not the main one. The freedom to choose what to think and how to feel.

Transcending our humanity means to exercise this freedom.

Transcending our humanity means we don't deny that we have fear, that we feel unstable, that we might even feel panic. We accept that,

but

consciously we choose to think of the things we are grateful for,

consciously we choose to count our blessings,

consciously we choose to surrender to call of the moment rather than struggle with it, consciously we make our home environment a happy one, by playing music, sharing jokes, laughing together, & sharing nourishing meals together.

This is where we go from being a victim of circumstances to victor of our surroundings.

Now you choose.

-28

*T*o surrender means to be present to the call of the moment with trust, and faith, understanding that every moment carries its own call.

That presence sometimes calls for action and sometimes inaction,

sometimes for words spoken and sometimes silence,

sometimes play and sometimes for observation.

We wrongly assume that surrender means to stand back, to do nothing, to just allow things to be as they are.

On the contrary, surrender never stands back. It is always alive, always curious to what's coming up and fully present to what's showing up.

Surrender leaves behind struggle, friction, resistance and conflict with its surroundings. Instead it uses the energy, will, with great desire to be aware of the now, for its in this now that gifts of self, wisdom, faith can be exercised.

Never underestimate the growth, beauty, and development of self that's present in each moment, no matter the circumstances, simply by surrendering to the call of the moment.

For today allow the friction to dissolve, be aware, be fully present, surrender, and allow your inner gifts to flow through you.

Then watch the beauty of the moment unfold, even amongst all the chaos.

-29

It is 38 years that the Israelites have moved about the desert, with leadership of Moshe Rabbeinu and complete awareness of presence and guidance of G-d.

They are very close to the land of Israel and have to move through the Edomite kingdom to gain access. The Edomite reject them and don't allow them to move through.

As a result the Israelite have to retreat.

They become impatient, despondent, wary, and discouraged. They start blaming G-d, complain about their food(manna), their misfortunes, and start questioning the leadership.

Because of their complaining, & ungratefulness for constant protection, food(manna), water, cloud of glory, they temporarily loose spiritual protection, and the poisonous snakes that were always present in the desert attack the nation

(First time in 38 years).

What heals them from the snake bite?

H-Shem orders Moshe to make a copper rod with a snake coiled around it(the sign for medicine). Whoever looks up to the copper stick would be healed.

The lesson for us:

1. Don't judge the place your in too fast. They were in it for 38 years already, yet they judged it too fast. The challenging situations or setbacks of our life might take one day, might take a week, might take longer. Never judge the place that you are at. You have to wait to see where the journey takes you.

2. We must be diligent to not resort to complaining when things don't work out the way we want to. We have to be solution oriented rather than magnifying what's wrong.

I want to be clear here, that being in pain, whether physical, spiritual, emotional or mental is not a form of complain, and must always always be addressed.

Complain is when all the other blessings become naught in presence of that difficulty or setback.

3. Constantly focusing on setback, misfortune, and dwelling on it, makes us loose our balance, our connection, and we loose our inspiration and insight to move forward, hence the loss of spiritual protection.

4. By gazing upward we are raising our own head, standing tall, and not in a failure position, which is hunched over. G-d never wants us to take the stance of a failure, for in his vocabulary that doesn't exist.

5. Our healing is within the problem itself. The healing came as they gazed upwards towards H-Shem at the copper snake. Our healing comes when we gaze upwards towards G-d, elevating the problem/setback/disappointment to a level where it even shines with brightness, like the copper rod.

For today:

Let's not judge the place this world is at, for we have no idea of the light that might come after it.

Let's not complain of all the discomforts we might be facing, for we might fall short of gratitude for all blessings we do have.

Let's stand tall as a community and know that as we connect together through prayer we are gaining spiritual protection for our community and world at large.

Let's gaze heavenward and elevate this situation to a state of healing.

-30

*T*he caterpillar becomes a chrysalis for the sake of becoming a butterfly.

The caterpillar is very happy going about it's business, eating leaf, going from leaf to leaf, however, it knows in order to become a butterfly it must confine itself, regroup itself, rearrange itself. It knows it must give up everything it has known up to that point, voluntarily put itself into a cocoon, dissolve all its body parts and fully rearrange itself. It does it with patience because instinctually it knows that it must go through that process for metamorphosis to take place. Without it, it would just be a caterpillar, never experiencing itself as the beautiful butterfly that can fly, and enjoy a wider range of movement than the caterpillar ever dreamt of.

Is it possible all of this confinement is a pre-requisite to our metamorphosis?

Is it possible we have finished being a caterpillar, and by Divine intervention we have been pushed into paradigm of chrysalis?

Is it possible that for us to enter into a whole fresh, elevated paradigm we need to be in a cocoon?

If so, we have to do our part in the process of transformation.

We have to give up all areas of our life that's not in alignment with our soul and Divine consciousness.

We have to fully embrace the moment, for it is in utilizing this moment to its highest potential, that holds the key to greater Divinity to enter our lives.

We have to begin our day with faith in where we are, and end our day with faith that we are about to enter into a zone of light never experienced before.

Yes, we will go through this, however, the call of the moment is to grow through this.

PS. The caterpillar becoming chrysalis is NOT a punishment, but rather a necessary step in its evolvement to a butterfly.

-31

Prophetess Miriam and million of Jews were at the peak of slavery in Egypt. Pharaoh had ordered that they make the structures on quick sand with no raw materials, and yet they had to deliver nothing less than as if they had the raw materials, otherwise they would be punished.

What is Miriam doing?

She is making tambourine, for she knew that proceeding this hardship, is going to be great light of redemption. She was making the tambourine to sing, dance and greet redemption into their lives.

She had her eye on redemption and the light that was about to come rather than the darkness of slavery that they were at the moment.

She also asked all the other women to do the same.

The women of that era showed tremendous amount of faith, for they didn't become embeshed with the darkness and challenge of the time, something for which G-d acknowledges them for in the desert many years later(later on this).

These tambourines were used to sing, and dance to G-d as they were crossing Red Sea some years later.

Prophetess Miriam has paved the way for us that for all times, in all dire situations whether on a personal level or national level, we have the capacity and power to greet the light even in midst of great darkness.

She has given us the fortitude to see beyond the moment, and the strength to do what we need to do in the moment to invite that light into our lives.

As the heirs to our heritage, the time calls on us to do the same. To, metaphorically speaking, make instruments of celebration, and joy. Not tomorrow and not when this thing is over, today, in midst of all this chaos.

It might be challenging, however, it's with in our capacity and the promise is that even the littlest act of faith will never go unnoticed by G-d.

Let's start making our tambourines.

-32

The first commandment states:

"I am H-Shem, your G-d, who has taken you out of land of Egypt, from house of slavery"

The first commandment is more like a statement than a commandment. It's not telling us to do or not to do, like the other 9 commandments. It's just giving us a statement.

Everything in our life needs to start with this statement.

Why?

G-d could have used the space on the tablets to say how he created heaven and earth, how he created the stars and galaxies, how he created the universes, but no he uses the space to say how He is the One and only One who is involved, deeply involved in taking us out of Egypt.

Egypt in Hebrew is Mitzrayim which comes from the word Mitzar, meaning tight and narrow.

Egypt, metaphorically, is a place of challenge, darkness, tightness. G-d is the one who takes out of the narrowness, out of the darkness, out of the challenge.

He involves Himself with every aspect of our lives, whether it's in joy or sadness, whether it's in elevation or desperation,

Whether it's in darkness or light.

He is right here, next to us, holding our hand, guiding us and taking us the next level of our journey.

The first commandment is a statement of Faith, and a testimony to tremendous amount of love G-d has for every single one of us.

Every part of our journey begins and ends with this statement.

It is imperative that we feel G-d right next to us, embracing us in his light, knowing the challenge we are going through, strengthening us with his love, & blessing us with his wisdom.

He wants us to know this with all our heart, before we even attempt to keep any other commandments.

All we need to do is to be open to it.

-33

The Torah begins with first day of creation.

On the first day G-d says "let there be light. "

The Rebbe said the it could also be read as "It should become light".

All this world, even the darkness, should become a source of light.

On that first day, G-d imbued the universe with the possibilities of light in every aspect of existence, including our lives, the circumstances of our lives, and people in our lives.

Our purpose then is to reveal this light in every aspect of creation.

How do we reveal this light within creation?

When we take note of the beauty of everything we see and touch.

When we are grateful for every step we take into every moment, no matter how it's presenting itself.

When we extract the good out of the situation.

When we see the good in a person even if they are acting otherwise.

When we see the possibility of growth in hardship.

When we see G-D's love in every breath, no matter how hard the circumstances might be.

When we love another for the sake of loving their soul.

When we are grateful for the seasons, the winters, and springs of our lives.

Then the moment and the circumstances thank us, for all along they have been waiting for us to redeem them out of darkness and reveal their light.

Your purpose being actualized.

-34

The brain is an organ designed for change.

Up to just a few short years ago, there was the idea that brain cannot change in any fundamental way. This dogma is completely wrong. It is now known that we can use the brain capabilities to change and enhance. Scientists have discovered that daily activities can harness this powerful ability.

Exercise, walking, aerobics, eating healthy, they all help maintain brain health and function. However, mediation, prayer, cognitive contemplation, hope, compassionate thinking, has actually been shown to trigger neurons to fire.

Thoughts and ideas that are maintained consistently over time cause long-term changes in the brain chemistry and function, making new pathways that eventually lead to change that's seen through behavior and action.

Use this precious time that you are home, to harness the brain capability by putting aside sometime to meditate, contemplate, allow for hope and compassionate thinking to expand in your consciousness, and just test the results for yourself in how you are being, how you are reacting and how you are responding.

Remember not only is the brain designed for change, but so are we.

-35

3,332 years ago exactly to date, G-d commanded Moshe to tell the Jewish people to sanctify the new moon.

The people at that point hadn't left Egypt, they were in midst of witnessing the last plagues that befell Egypt, they are not sure exactly when they will be leaving, and yet G-d gives them the first commandment in midst of all the chaos.

Bless the new moon, celebrate Rosh Chodesh.

Why now? Why not wait after they have left Egypt? Why the first commandment?

Why even before the 10 commandments?

G-d was teaching them and all generations to follow, that in order to leave slavery, you have to be master over time, not time be master over you.

Slavery is defined as any condition, habit, psychological mindset, emotional hang up, that confines you.

Before you embark on journey, you have to know that nothing chains you, nothing binds you. From that day forth G-d instilled in all our souls the ability to bring holiness into our surroundings even if we find ourselves in midst of chaos.

No thing binds you, not even time.

G-d Also showed Moshe the secret of the darkness that is right before the crescent moon of Rosh Chodesh.

In that darkness no light of moon is apparent to our eyes. The moon is completely hidden from vision.

The secret?

Even though it's dark to our eyes with no moon to be seen, the moon at its darkest is at its closest angle to the sun.

From there it's gets its light for its next cycle of birth and rebirth.

Our lesson:

Today is Rosh Chodesh Nissan.

We stand with Moshe, and all those Israelites who were still slaves at that point, blessing the new moon.

Today we break free of spiritual confinements. We bless the new moon, inviting the energy of renewal, and rebirth, understanding that any growth and birth is preceded by blackness.

We have also been shown the secret through Moshe, the blackness is exactly where our soul is closest to its sun, G-d, the point where rebirth happens….hence the miracle of crescent moon.

Bless the time

Bless the newness

Bless the rebirth

And rest in the fact that in order to get to crescent moon, you need to go through the darkened moon.

−36

*C*onfidence and humility seem to be exact opposites, yet confidence is found within the truly humble.

Moses was and is the most humble man, yet he had the confidence to stand in front of Pharaoh and demand he let the Jewish people go. He had the confidence to argue for sake of Jewish people with G-d. He had the confidence to stay on a mountain and be in communion with G-d for 80 days and night, till the nation was granted forgiveness. He had the confidence to be the channel of all that was transmitted through out the 40 years in desert.

Where did this confidence come from?

The confidence he had was not in himself and his abilities but that he is the agent of G-d.

Self-confidence is confidence in one's ability which is limited.

However, if we trust that G-d has sent us here for a purpose and we are his agent on earth, then that confidence has no limitation in what it can accomplish.

Humility is the ability to go beyond self.

Confidence is the ability to act on that.

This is a true leader, humble before G-d and the people, yet confident to move forward and do what needs to be done.

We are all born with the capacity to lead, to have humility and confidence to do what's required of us, knowing that what's required of us might change momentarily.

This moment in time is upon us to lead our own self and our own home. It's not about the world out there, but about the world inside. We can move forth with humility and yet confident that we can do what's required of us at this moment and we will be successful in doing G-d's calling here on earth.

-37

Our soul possesses many properties, some of which remain dormant, till the situation arises that the quality could be awakened, and tapped into. The awakening requires a conscious effort.

Some of the qualities are:

Resilience

Buoyancy

Endurance

Patience

Adaptability

Inner balance

The ability to shift

The ability to elevate

The ability to transform

The maturity of our soul relies on all of its qualities being awakened and brought into physical reality.

We are all going through a time that has thrown us off from our natural habitat, in our thoughts, in our daily actions, and in our daily activities.

Added to this, some of us are in unexpected situations, of loved ones being sick with this virus, or even ourselves at this point, some of us are in a financial bind, some of us have conditions that contracting the virus could potentially be detrimental, & some of us have elderly parents that are at high risk.

These all bring up much fear and rightly so, especially when we see ourselves in a helpless situation, where we can be of no help under these circumstances.

The fear is valid.

There is another route.

The conscious effort to tap into the above soul powers, and the time requires of us to do just that.

We will never come fully into ourselves, fully into who we are and who we can be, if in challenging times we don't utilize our G-dly given gifts.

Who we are is defined by who we become under pressure and challenge.

Choose a different path if you sit in fear, not only because you can, but because it's the calling of the moment, and an expression of your soul.

Tap into the above qualities and be a greater G-fly expression of all you have been.

Yes, it's possible, and yes you can.

38

The pomegranate has a great significance in Judaism, it represents the 613 mitzvot that we each carry in potential.

Saying it in a different way, it represents the many paths of connection that we each possess, in potential.

The pomegranate is covered with the thick skin, only to be seen what's inside when the skin is cut open.

All those seeds, each one of them can become a tree once it's planted.

There are two major acts that take place here, the skin being broken, and the seed/s being planted.

It represents the many hidden potentials we all have. Our skin is cut open by either we start looking inside, or somehow circumstances bring us to look inside.

We have many paths of connection available to us, but we must at least choose one, plant it, nurture it, be patient with it, till we bring just one of them into actualization.

We are all in such time, the conditions of outside ourselves are bringing us to break open our skin and look inside.

Choose one potential, recognize it within yourself, start nurturing it.

There are many many paths of connection,

Prayer

Meditation

Keeping kosher, conscious eating

Keeping Shabbat, conscious presence in time

Words that illuminate the heart

Music

Having frequent conversations with G-d

Expressing Faith & Trust

Expressing love

Compassionate action

Being present

Surrender

And so many more....

We are all the above in potential.

It's time we recognize all that we are, all that we hold, and all that needs to be actualized.

We are the pomegranate that's breaking open. Now, it's up to us to plant.

-39

*O*ur world is dynamic, complex, & interdependent.

The butterfly effect, is a term used to emphasize how a minute occurrence can lead to significant outcome, how small things can have impact on a complex system.

To illustrate the butterfly effect, the theory imagines a butterfly flapping its wings on one side of the world and typhoon happening on other side of the world.

A proverb written by Benjamin Franklin many years before this theory, is a beautiful illustration of something tiny can bring about a significant event,

For want of a nail the shoe was lost

For want of a shoe the horse was lost

For want of a horse the rider was lost

For want of a rider the battle was lost

For want of a battle the kingdom was lost

And all for a want of a horseshoe nail

It used to be thought that big events change the world. The things that bring change in actuality are the tiny events.

If we ever had doubt, we can see with events of past few months, how a person ingesting some food in a different part of the world, causes major health crisis in the rest of the world.

If this is true on a physical level, which it is, how much more so on a spiritual level.

A tiny change in the way we converse could have significant effect in the world.

A tiny change in our daily behavior, could bring about monumental change in the world.

A tiny change in expression of our love, could have consequential outcome in the world.

Imagine a tiny change in your behavior could subsequently change the direction of the world.

What if the whole world is waiting for you to make that tiny change?

-40

When light is beamed into a space, you start seeing more clearly, you also see all the places that need cleaning, the cob webbs, the dirt, the dust.

You start seeing more clearly what's around you, what is old and needs to go, what needs to be thrown away, so there is space for the new, what needs to be restored, and what needs to be salvaged.

During month of Nissan, the world is infused with more light, we automatically do spring cleaning and start getting rid of chametz to enter into freedom.

It is possible that G-d has infused so much light into the universe at this time, that we have no choice but see. He has created a scenario where in the solitude of our own space, we have to look and look clearly. We are able to see what gifts we possess, but also to see what needs to be cleaned up.

It's clean up time. Cleaning up the dust bunnies of our psyche, clearing the stuck emotions, throwing out the outdated stories we tell ourselves about ourselves and others, making space for the new.

Making space for the truth of who we really are, making room for the authentic self.

H-Shem has put us into a place, where it's a time to major inner cleaning.

As frightening as this crisis might be, it is possible that this will usher us into the spring of our lives, with a whole refreshed look at ourselves and life.

After all the cleaning, dusting, throwing away, restoring of self, H-Shem in his infinite kindness is giving us the opportunity see our authentic self, and is bringing us into a whole new reality that before it seemed impossible....a world that sees itself connected and united.

Light is here, greater and brighter than before.

Let us use this light to see clearer than before, to bring wisdom into our own lives and the world, and together in health and safety walk into a new era and a whole refreshed consciousness.

−41

We are dualistic beings made of completely two different paradigms, body and soul.

The body wants its desires met, the soul wants its light to shine, the body is limited in its expression, the soul is limitless in its potential, the body knows itself in time and space, the soul is timeless and not limited to physical space.

Our whole life is a dance between these two paradigms and our wholeness comes about as a result of harmony between these two states.

The fact is the soul needs the body to share its light, to give it form and expression. The body needs the soul to give it life, breath, inspiration, insight and wisdom. It's a perfect partnership. In this partnership both ask to be nourished and nurtured.

Why nourish the soul?

It is imprinted within it the purpose/s for which you are present on this earth at this time. It has the wisdom of knowing how best to dance with circumstances of life and create balance, it has the vision to know when to step forth and when to stay still, and it has the light that shines on a stormy day that illuminates the path.

Don't be shy with nurturing your soul, for you might just shy away from your light and purpose.

Nourish both, body and soul, and watch this beautiful dance of knowing and expression to unfold before you.

-42

***F**reedom comes with responsibility and accountability*

Freedom is the maturity of a conscious person who is not enslaved to most basic desires nor is enslaved to a societal ideology. The person bears sole responsibility, for having authorship for this freedom, knowing that the very basis of freedom of choice, is a choice between being enslaved and being free.

We could be enslaved to different things, thought patterns, emotional memories, addictions like shopping, alcohol, smoking, and yes addiction to worrying. We could be enslaved to distorted reality, low self-esteem, self-obsession, and self-pity.

Freedom is never a one time thing, but an evolving ongoing process.

This Shabbat, is Shabbat Hagadol, the Shabbat that blesses the coming week of Passover, a time when G-d with pure love takes us out of slavery and into freedom.

This Shabbat blesses our ability to break all our chains free, and with G-d's kindness leap over all forms of limitations.

At this time that major crisis is looming over us, and we are bound to our homes with many not well, and some in hospitals, where is our freedom, and what is our responsibility?

Each and every single one of us bears the responsibility not only for ourselves but also for the entire nation, to move from a state of bondage of fear to state of freedom of faith. We have the blessing from above this Shabbat. We have to access the deepest places of our soul and bring out into reality our faith.

This is the calling of our time, and we all bear the responsibility both for self and for each other.

-43

*H*ave the fortitude to walk away from anything that diminishes your light

Once a year we are infused with courage, insight and strength to leave behind all things that suppress our true identity, a soul with purpose.

H-Shem extends his hands and asks us to hold it, for he will lead us into the zone of miraculous.

However, we must do our part.

We must walk away from all we have known, the habits of mind, the voices, the voice of not me, why me, the voice of not now, the voice of I have no strength, the limitations we have imprisoned ourselves in, and walk into a world that's unknown, unpredictable, might even be barren like a desert, but it's the zone of miraculous.

This once a year event, is on passover.

G-d held our hand and we followed him into the desert, and as a gift, overnight we went from a state of slavery to state of prophecy.

Our part, walk away.

Walk away in haste.

The Israelites left Egypt in haste. Why? Because if we wait, we think twice.

Even though it's slavery, it's all we know.

Walk away in haste.

If you don't,

It diminishes you.

It lowers your standards.

It sacrifices your soul.

It numbs your purpose.

It makes you into a slave.

On night of Passover, you have the fortitude to walk away from all those limitations that diminish your light.

Hold G-d hand and walk away.

-44

Ice, water, vapor, are made up of exactly the same thing, yet they look nothing alike.

They are in completely different states of existence, solid, liquid, gas. The difference between them, heat.

The degree of heat determines the state in which water molecules find themselves in.

The same is true of us, human beings.

We can exist in different states depending on the heat, or life force, applied to our life.

Sometimes, the amount of heat is determined by the circumstances outside of us, and sometimes the amount of heat comes from the conditioning, and thought process, inside of us.

We can find ourselves in a state of ice, where our life is cold, has no movement, flow, no creativity, feels heavy, disconnected, disjointed, and somewhat unapproachable.

Or

We can find ourselves in a state of fluidity, joyful, flowing, life giving, sharing, open, connecting, buoyant, and the ability to flow around and through obstacles, like water moving around rocks.

Both can exist within us at the same time.

The difference between water and us, we have a soul, and a conscious mind that even if outside circumstances are cold and would turn us to ice, we, with our internal light and heat turn it to water.

All we need to do is turn our internal heat on.

What state do you find yourself in?

You feel disconnected, disjointed, disappointed, disheartened, dissatisfied?

Turn on your internal heat.

It's your G-d given gift, utilize it.

-45

The difference between Matzah and chametz is a hairs breath

When matzah and chametz are written in Hebrew, they both have two letters in common, mem and Tzadi. The letters that separate chametz from matzah is Chet and Hei. Chet and hei are very similar except an opening in letter hei, the difference being a hairs breath.

Right before Passover we do everything to get rid of chametz and during Passover we eat matzah, yet it seems that they are much closer than we imagine.

From slavery to freedom is a shift as small as a hairs breath.

What is Chet that contributes to chametz?

Why the obsession to get rid of chametz?

The Chet is written like a four sided square without the line on bottom.

It's closed in. It knows only itself. It knows only it's own walls. It has secured itself, so it can not be moved or effected. It has become a self within a made up self. It has no room to see another or to connect to another. It's walled in. Oh yes, there are many stories about these walls, many images about why they are there. These walls become the self-image. An image that one can become enslaved to.

Comes the Hei of matzah, it makes an opening in the Chet. It allows for movement, flexibility, connection.

It's matzah, flat, our purest self with no self made image, no walls, no stories.

The Hei just opens up space

It opens up space for possibilities

It opens up space to step into a more expanded paradigm

It opens up to invite another in

It opens up to invite H-Shem in

It has nothing to loose, for its flat, and bland

This blandness of self is called humility. In this is the greatest freedom. There is nothing holding on to it, or holding it back. It is free to become.

What's your self-image?

From slavery to redemption is only hairs breath away.

-46

Tonight, we walk into a vortex of time.
A time of miracles.

A time redemption.

A time of complete awareness of H-Shem presence.

A time of complete awareness of H-Shem love.

A time of movement from one state of being to another.

A time of complete surrender and Trust in H-Shem.

A time of being united.

A time of leaving our enslaved selves to our liberated selves.

A time of leaving our Egypts and self made Pharaohs.

The virtue of vortex is that you are in same exact energy, no matter if it happened last year or over 3,000 years ago.

Passover is not about tradition of remembering but rather experiencing and connecting to the same consciousness.

Everything we do on seder night is to connect us to that consciousness and sharpen our awareness to the energy of the moment.

Tonight as many of us sit alone at the Seder table, separated from our loved ones, we have a rare opportunity to consciously and intimately connect and be present in the vortex.

We are at a very important juncture in journey of human consciousness.

Let us fully connect with the miracles that are waiting for us to step into, the paradigm that's inviting us to step into, and with unity that we feel for each other, no matter how physically seperated we are, usher in a new era of human existence.

H-Shem himself is present with us tonight.

Not his angels, not his emissaries, but Himself. He himself embraces us with tremendous love, holds our hand and guides us to our collective destiny.

May the miracles of these moments bring healing to all who are not well and all those hospitalized.

Together, hand in hand, united and connected with each other at deepest level, embraced in H-Shem arms, we leap into an elevated paradigm.

Chag kosher Sameach.

-47

Matzah, the bread of faith proclaims: I am 100% committed with unhesitating action, constancy, patience, gratitude, love, receptivity and humility to the Divine plan that's waiting for us to step into, and I know with conviction that each day asks us to be present with laser sharp focus to the call of the day.

I am faith, I do not waiver in knowing that Divine providence guides and informs the events in our life and embraces us with His love to give us the knowledge and wisdom that every moment is part of the whole, and every action influences the whole.

I am faith, I do not waiver in my commitment. I am humbled to the guidance and love of Divine presence.

I am faith, I do not waiver.

−48

*W*hat would the rose be with out it's thorns?

What would the mountain peaks be without the valley?

What would trees be without rain?

What would light be without darkness?

What would faith be without fear?

H-Shem has created a world of paradoxes and dichotomies, where opposites exist simultaneously. They co-exist not to oppose each other, although it seems so on the surface, but rather if we choose, to enhance the beauty of that which is light and good.

Fear can be fear and need not be denied, however, it can enhance faith simultaneously.

Darkness can be darkness and need not be denied, however, it can magnify a flicker of light simultaneously.

All exists within simultaneously, the so called negative doesn't negate the positive but only enhances it, that is if we choose to.

Through our fear we get to greater faith.

Through our darkness we get to greater wisdom and light.

Through our thorns we get to the rose.

Don't be dismayed at darkness or at fear, use it to enhance your light and your faith.

Don't stop at the thorn, be patient for the rose.

-49

There is G-dliness in both heaven and earth.

Earth is G-dliness layered in obscurity.

G-d wants a world where He is even present in the layers of obscurity and it all depends on us to make his presence known.

We can unlayer the layers by,

A mind that seeks the knowledge of Divine Presence,

A heart that is compassionate, caring, kind, sensitive to others,

Action that is a reflection of mind and heart, and moves forward with great faith, even though outside circumstances dictate otherwise.

On Thursday, we arrive in a vortex of time of opening of Red Sea, a miraculous event that saved the Jewish people from what seemed a dire situation, sandwiched between Pharoah's army and the Red Sea.

In an unprecedented turn of events, H-Shem tells Moshe, "why you pray to me, move forward". As they moved forward, into the water that is, the sea splits.

With splitting of the sea, the Israelites reached a level of prophecy that they say is greater that prophecies of Ezekiel.

The inner and outer world became one, they could see with clarity their connection to G-d, the heavenly spheres, their souls mission, and presence of G-d's light and love.

G-d's presence was known in the layers and there was no obscurity.

All of this came to be, because they did their part in partnership with G-d to bring the miracles about…moving forward.

We too, can tap into the miracles.

We can bridge heaven and earth, unlayering the layers, clearing the obscurity, making a space in this coarse physical earthiness for G-d and his miracles.

The secret, move forward.

Move forward with faith.

The catalyst for bringing about all these miracles is our action of taking our feet and walking into the unknown with faith, even though it looks like we might drown.

Move forward and you will know your mission.

Move forward and you gain clarity about your purpose.

Move forward and you will see miracles along the way.

Move forward and bring miracles of heaven unto earth.

Move forward and make space for G-d's knowledge, and love to enter the obscurity and opaqueness of earth.

Move forward.

−50

*E*verything in this universe is informed of its duty and purpose, everything from the smallest one cell organism to the planets and stars.

Nature knows exactly when to do and not to do.

The trees know innately when to blossom and when to shed leaves.

The animals know innately what to do and what's in its nature.

The spider knows how to weave it's Webb.

The butterfly knows how to change from one stage to another.

The ants know who is the leader and who is the worker.

The birds know when to migrate and where to.

The fish know how to swim and which direction to move.

The earth knows when to tilt and how fast to rotate.

The sun knows to shine.

The moon knows to rotate around the earth.

Everything knows of its position, what it's meant to do, there is no question for nature.

The only force within nature that doesn't know and needs to figure itself out is, human.

The human being is born with purpose but it needs to be revealed, and needs to be figured out. In process of coming to know there is much struggle within, there is confusion, till the path becomes clear, even if it does become clear.

The human is unsure of itself, questions its direction, its position, and ponders of its existence.

Why is this so?

Because the human being is expected to grow. We are not meant to come and leave exactly as we came.

What's innately in us is to grow, to evolve consciously, to elevate beyond that which the eye sees and the senses feel, and most importantly to connect and establish relationship with our creator.

G-d has created us as part of nature but has given us the ability to rise above nature.

G-d has given us innate characteristics but given us the ability of Mastery.

G-d has given us the sense of navigation within our circumstances and given us the ability to redefine, re-evaluate, re-establish ourselves within the context of our circumstances.

G-d has given us the wisdom to find the light within and how to shine it without.

G-d has given us the power of love, to reshape reality.

G-d has even given us the power to effect spiritual spheres with our choices that is not so apparent to our senses.

There are times when these qualities flow through us and there are times that circumstances can probe these qualities out of us.

We are in such circumstances.

The circumstances themselves inform part of our purpose.

Let us use it wisely, and become a force greater than nature by our growth and mastery.

−51

The eagle at about age 30 has to make a painful decision, die or regenerate through a painful process of plucking its feathers and knocking off its beak. The process can last 4-5 months, however, it gains another 30-40 years of life.

There is a powerful lesson in this:

We as humans also need to go through a process of shedding, letting go, getting rid of habits that no longer serve, getting rid of thought process that's unhealthy, and getting rid of toxic behavior.

It's a process of re-evaluation and recalibration. It can be painful, but if we don't do it a part of us is at the risk of dying.

Through the process of re-evaluation and resetting, we become rejuvenated and enlivened. It takes time, effort of plucking old feathers, energy to knock the old beak, but if we keep at it, we gain life and vigor.

The eagle chooses to extend its life.

We too must choose life.

-52

The book of Job describes the prophet Job as an upright and wholesome man.

Job has a prosperous life, with a great family, wealth, and honor.

On one misfortune day he looses everything....his children, his wealth, crops, land and servants.

He also gets inflicted with a disease that leaves him with fresh wounds all over his body.

Three of his friends come to visit to comfort him. However, at some point they get into ideological discussion as why G-d has brought about this disaster unto Job.

One suggested that his kids weren't righteous, the other suggested that he must have done something to get such reaction from G-d. They went on theological discussion as to the nature of G-d and why he does what he does.

Job gets upset at them and refuses all their arguments, for he knows he is upright.

He turns to G-d and demands an answer.

Why is this happening to me?

G-d's answer to Job:

"Where were you when I laid the earth's foundation? Tell if you know.

Who set its dimensions?

Who stretched a line over it?

Who laid it's cornerstone?

Did you ever in your life command the morning, or teach the dawn its place?

Have you penetrated the hidden depths of sea?

What is the path where the light dwells? Tell, if you know it. " Job 38:4-17

Job responds to G-d,

"I am deficient, what can I answer you? I spoke once and I will not speak up again"

G-d chastised the friends for speaking in that manner to Job, and asked them to ask Job to pray for them so G-d forgives them.

Job was healed and was blessed with even more kids, wealth and honor.

We don't know G-D's ways.

We don't know why things happen as they happen.

We can't even fathom or begin to understand the unfolding of events.

Everything is interconnected and interlaced from the inception of earth till eternity.

We weren't there when G-d laid the foundation of earth.

We can't assume that if something negative is happening is a punishment, or G-D's anger.

We can't point a finger and say you did it, and so it's deserved.

We simply don't know.

We do know that His providence is in everything.

We do know that for G-d there is a reason, however, for us we can't even fathom to understand.

We know that G-d wants us to be so deeply bound to him that he will hold and carry us through calamities.

Like Job, we can say, I will speak up no more. I trust you with all I have, with my soul, body, family, wealth and honor.

Like Job we turn our questions of why into gratitude and appreciation for all life is, for His presence and providence in every aspect of existence.

With that Trust, we are healed in his embrace, and we become a vessel for blessings to come forth.

−53

G-d Created man with power of mouth, the power of words, and the ability to create worlds by utterance of words and speech.

Words emanate from breath that passes through the vocal cords, and out from the mouth.

Words use the breath that is the source of life, the vitality of our being, to communicate that which is part of our inner being to outside of self.

Words are like music being played on the string cords of instruments.

Once music is made and played, it remains as part of the greater eternal symphony, and becomes an integral part of the vibratory structure of the universe.

There are two chapters of Torah dedicated to a disease called tzaaras, that is caused by words misused and abused.

On the one hand, the misuse of words is the misuse of breath of life. It is taking that breath and through our own conscious mind directing it on a path of destruction. The very breath that gives us life, is used to destroy life.

Added to that, words have a vibration that once uttered can never be retrieved and change the vibration of the universe as small as it might be, forever.

The remedy for Tzaaras in Torah, quarantine for 14 days, after which time the Cohen has the power, again by the use of his mouth, to declare clean or unclean.

Imagine, every time you utter one word, you are changing the vibration of the entire universe for all times.

Imagine, you have the power to make beautiful music with words that eternally echo in the universe.

Imagine, by utterance of your words you can bring someone goodness out or you can bring out their darkest shadows.

Imagine, the redemption of another is in your mouth and in your words.

Imagine, the tremendous responsibility you carry, not only for self but the entire direction of universe.

As conscious beings, are we not responsible for ourselves, our families, communities and humanity at large?

Are we not responsible to bring healing and reveal goodness?

This responsibility lies in the power of our mouth.

Use the breath of life to create life, to be part of the creative force of universe that aligns itself with healing, love and connection.

-54

DNA, is a molecule composed of two chains that coil around each other carrying genetic instruction for development, growth, function, and reproduction.

DNA contains four building blocks, adenine, cytosine, guanine, thymine.

The order and sequence of these building blocks is the instructions that the cells carry to become what it becomes.

Every single cell has the same DNA, yet every cell knows of its function, what's expected of it, the different hormones and enzymes that it needs to make, even different cell structure to be able to carry its function.

The liver cell looks different than the brain cell, yet it carries the same DNA.

The heart cell looks different than the colon cell, yet has the same DNA.

Each part is aware of the whole. The whole is dependent on its part, and the part is dependent on the whole.

If each part fails its function, it has effect on all other parts.

Our spiritual makeup is the same way.

The whole is dependent on the one. Each single one carries the genetic makeup of the whole, yet has its own function. If there is a dysfunction with one, the whole gets effected.

We collectively make the body.

Each one of us works independently of the other, having different talents and capacities. Each one of us has a different function or purpose in this world. However, the whole system is dependent on it.

Each one of us carries the whole.

Each one of us independent, has free will, can make thousand different choices, and yet each has a ripple effect on the whole beyond our comprehension.

Just like the DNA sequencing, that to naked eye is unreadable, our spiritual coding to the naked eye is unreadable.

However, we see the reflection of our spiritual coding in our behavior, temper, awareness, consciousness, and our spiritual growth.

They used to think that DNA is set, is unchangeable, and we are at its mercy, now they know that our actions, what we eat, and what we think can actually change our genetic makeup and this change can be passed down to generations through the change in DNA.

Our spiritual DNA, works the same way, what we do consciously, the choices we make with awareness, our faith, our trust, our patience, our love, our compassion, our growth, becomes part of our spiritual DNA, that gets passed down as heritage to generations to come.

Each of our actions effects the whole.

Each thought effects the whole.

We carry the total information for the whole, yet we have our own task and job to do.

The whole depends on us to do that which we are here to do, otherwise the whole suffers.

Become the best of you, for the whole depends on you.

Become the best of you, for you will effect its direction and its genetic makeup for generations to come.

-55

*J*acob's ladder in Jacob's dream, is connected to earth on one end, and the other reaches the heavens.

The steps on the ladder represent the different levels of consciousness.

Every level is unto itself important for its a chain.

The ladder represents our spiritual journey.

Our soul is having an earthly existence, and yet it's always connected to the heavens.

We ourselves, might see ourselves on step one of the ladder, we might only be aware of ourselves and our capacity on that first step, however, our soul's connection is always there, the steps always there, our soul always connected to top and nothing can sever it or take it away.

The top of the ladder, represents the soul's purity, dignity, quintessential spark of self, and under all circumstances it remains connected and pure.

The spiritual ladder has flexibility like rope.

If you move the rope from bottom, it's vibration reaches all the way to top.

Wherever you find yourself at, whatever step you find yourself at, you make a movement from that place and it causes a vibration and movement through out the rope.

We, sometimes have clarity, strength, confidence to move up the ladder, and sometimes we feel otherwise.

The ladder teaches us, do not despair.

Your connection is always there, your purity, your essence always connected to G-d. It doesn't matter what step you see yourself at, the ladder is always there.

One movement from you, no matter at what level and the vibration is felt through out.

One movement, sometimes that's all the strength we have.

And sometimes that's all it's asking of us, one movement.

-56

*W*e are all born as originals, we must make sure that after 120 we don't leave as copies.

As social beings, we like to fit in, to be validated for who we are, be recognized, be better than, higher than, more than.

Month of Iyar, which today and tomorrow is the Rosh Chodesh of, teaches us that each one of us has unique inner light, and this is the month to not only get connected to it, but also to reveal it, so it shines through us.

In this we are originals, each one of us having an inner light that expresses itself through our personalities, our choices, our consciousness and our awareness.

Having 100% confidence in this inner essence gives the person the validation it needs. There is no other validation that's needed, no other trying to fit in, no trying to look a certain way or have the need to be recognized.

In this knowledge, all sense of comparison disappears, as each inner light has its own finger print and can never look or be like anyone else's.

This also allows and give space for others to be the expression of their unique light.

This is the greatest form of love.

This is how we enter into a soul filled life,

Confidence of our inner light, confidence of our connection to G-d, confidence that the only thing that can dim or brighten our light is our own consciousness.

Chodesh Iyar is also connected to healing.

What greater healing than bringing back all external energies that we spend looking and giving power to outside of self, and taking all that energy to heal from within, to shine from within, to illuminate from within, making room for strengthening of our inner light's connection to G-d's light.

Drop all forms of comparison, leave behind all forms of validation, and spend the next month polishing your inner light.

Be confident in your uniqueness and don't allow it to be compromised for sake of fitting in.

-57

*T*rusting G-d with all aspects of life, requires surrender and humility.

Surrender is the ability to say, I may not know why things are as they are, and why things have evolved the way they have, but know that G-d knows his ways and his ways are perfect. Every moment as it's presenting itself is perfectly aligned with Divine plan, and it's for me to work with, use, shape and transform.

From human condition, we can never have the big picture and see the bigger puzzle that's being put together.

The greater we enter into surrender consciousness, the greater we are able to see G-d's hand and daily miracles in everyday life, somethings which would have gone unnoticed before.

Humility in Hebrew comes from root word, Hoda'ah, which means to thank.

Humility should not be equated with weakness and lack of self-esteem, but rather having the insight and inner knowing to say Thank you to G-d, and being grateful. It's being able to stand back from stories of life, the hurt and pain, and see the point of gratitude, finding light within the darkness, and verbalizing it.

It's the ability to shift focus from self, to outside of self, with understanding that you are here for a higher purpose, not just satisfying your own needs.

Humility and surrender are twins that allow for Divine light to flow through, even when things look dire and dark.

These twins also allow for presence of mind in the moment, agility of spirit, focus of mind, for its not using mental, emotional and spiritual energies to fight what is.

It invites serenity and peace to the moment.

Let us surrender today to all that is, being humble in thanking G-d for all the good that there is, and use the energies that's available to infuse joy, love and compassion into the space of our life.

Let us find good in the seeming dark places of life, and see the miracles unfold before us.

-58

*T*he journey to a thousand miles starts with the first step.

We are all on a journey called life. Each moment presenting itself with its own unique gifts. Each moment a stepping stone to the next.

In this journey we can't possibly judge the moment, and say it's for naught, since we don't have the vision to see the whole journey. If the moment is part of our life, then it has importance, even though in our eyes it looks otherwise.

Each moment is unique unto itself and is also pregnant with future moments.

The way this moment is being feed, nourishes and nurtures or creates imbalance for the potential moments waiting to be born and stepped into.

The moment, our soul, our lens through which we see the moment, our emotions, our mindset, all interact with each other at the same time to create what gets created and what gets born.

The question that we must ask ourselves then is, who do I want to give birth to?

The moment will do what the moment must do, to present itself.

We also must do what we can do in the moment to give birth to itself.

This moment is a stepping stone to the rest of our lives. This moment is pregnant with the future moments of our lives.

How we define, who we want to give birth to, creates the quality of interaction within this moment.

Who you want to give birth to?

Honor the moment, nurture the soul in the moment, align yourself to the journey, and be part of the creative process of perpetually birthing yourself into existence.

*E*chad-one, and Ahava-love, have the same numerical value, 13.

In Judaism words that have same numerical value, are intrinsically connected.

Echad-one, is declared everyday by saying Shema. G-d is one in heaven and on earth. He is one in the spiritual realm and physical realm and permeates in every aspect of existence.

He is one with it, and everything that exists is one with Him.

Everything in nature resonates with His oneness, the sun and moon, the birds, the fish, the oceans, the trees, the animals, everything except the human consciousness.

G-d gave us free will, and He desires that we connect to His oneness through our own free will and choice.

How can this oneness be revealed through our consciousness?

LOVE

Love is most powerful force of existence.

It's not seen and yet is seen.

It's not tangible and yet very tangible.

It doesn't have a voice, yet it speaks the loudest.

It doesn't have choice, yet it becomes the highest choice.

Divine oneness can only be complete within our own consciousness, only if we are able to love and love fully.

Divine oneness is Divine love.

Love everything and everyone.

Let love become your language.

Clear your heart from all the obstacles that stand in way of fully loving.

Clear your mind from all the walls that stand in way of seeing everything through the lens of oneness.

Become a conduit for Divine love to flow through you, and be the consciousness that expresses Divine oneness, in all that you do and all that you are.

-60

*A*braham was 75 years old, when he was commanded to leave Mesopotamia.

G-d tells him, lech lecha, translated as go to yourself. The verse reads,

"Go to yourself from your land, your relatives, your father's house to the land I show you".

He was commanded to leave the space of idol worship into holy space.

At some point in our lives we are all commanded to do a Lech lecha.

We are guided to leave the place we know, the place that limits us, the place that attaches us to idols of the time, the place that hides our light and essence, into a holy space, a space that knows G-d, and knows the essence of self.

It seems that G-d is commanding

"Lech lecha" on us.

Go to yourself, go inside yourself, and separate yourself from everything you know, the place you work, your friends, and your immediate family.

Lech lecha from a space of familiarity and limitation to space of curiosity and holiness.

Go to yourself, to the inner space that I show you.

We, as children of Abraham, and the bearers of his inheritance, trust the journey.

Just like him, we don't know the land that we are being lead to, however, we know that we are guided every step of the way and know that wherever we step into is part of the evolutionary process.

Lech lecha is a holy journey.

Don't allow mind chatter to get in the way of this holy journey.

We have all been called, and we are all being lead.

Go into yourself, and allow the journey to unfold itself while fully trusting the process.

Lech Lecha!

-61

*G*raphite and diamond have the same molecular structure,

Carbon.

However, they are drastically different.

Graphite is soft, like pencil, Diamond is hard.

Graphite is opaque, diamond is translucent.

Graphite is found in abundance, diamond is rare.

Graphite is found for the most part on surface of earth, diamond is found in depths of the earth.

Graphite is formed relatively quickly in comparison to diamond that takes 100,000s of years.

What turns graphite into diamond?

Heat, pressure and time.

We too, are the graphite that turns to diamonds.

This is the alchemy of self.

As we start our life journey, we can be very soft, being hurt by life circumstances, and others.

We are opaque. An opaque object doesn't absorb light. We too, can't fully absorb the light of H-Shem.

We are raw in our characteristics and plenty of us to go around, with not much depth.

We always have a choice. We can stay raw, soft, and opaque or with time, patience, pressure and pains of our life, transform into the translucent, magnificent diamond.

We can have brilliance that shines from within.

We can have luminescence.

We can have light interacting with our inner structure to sparkle.

We can be hard, yet be rare.

Don't let the pressures, & pains of life be wasted.

Allow them to be the reason and the ingredients of your alchemy.

It's our choice, graphite or diamond?

-62

Clouds give the appearance that they have no weight, since they float in air.

In actuality clouds in weight measurements are very heavy.

Average cloud weighs over a million Ibs.

It is paradox, how is it possible for cloud to be floating in air and yet carry so much weight?

Density

The density of clouds is lighter than density of air.

To the naked eye it seems impossible for anything to have lesser density than air, since air feels to have no density.

It's a paradox.

Paradoxes exist not only in physical realm but also in spiritual realm. What seems impossible to the naked eye, becomes very possible.

How can finite man, carry infinity?

How can mortal man become immortal?

How can the mundane become holy?

G-d tells Moshe, "speak to the entire assembly of children of Israel, you shall be holy, for I, H-Shem your G-d, am holy.

Parasha Kedoshim.

G-d then goes on to tell Moshe what actions and what kind of speeches make us holy.

G-d is telling us that we are capable of making every moment, even if it's mundane to the naked eye, holy.

It is a paradox that the finite human being can rise above the density of life, & become weightless.

It's a paradox that the mundane day to day, moment to moment, actions can elevate us and make us holy.

It's a paradox that right in our tongues by the words we speak we carry infinity.

To the naked eye, it doesn't seem logical.

It all lies within our choices.

No matter where we are, what we are doing, who we are and who we have been, this moment carries the difference between earthly and the sacred.

It's a paradox.

-63

There are four energetic bodies that are interacting and communicating with each other at all times.

Physical, emotional, mental, and spiritual.

Keeping a balance between all of them is the key for well-being.

In stressful times, we need to become more conscious of our feelings, thoughts, eating habits, & spiritual practice.

Here is a list of simple things we can do to keep us in balance.

Conscious breathing

Nature walks

Being well-hydrated

Eating healthy

Journal practice

Gratitude

Prayer

Acknowledging emotions, and making sure we are not stuck to the emotion, allowing it to move through. Remembering that emotions are exactly that, e-motion, energy in motion, and that we are not any particular emotion, it's just a certain energy that's moving through us.

Having a communication practice with G-d. Dialing G-d everyday to talk about anything and everything, our challenges, our thoughts, our uncertainties, our needs, wants and also everything that we have been blessed with, allowing the space for G-d to talk back to us, it's a conversation.

Becoming aware of our thoughts.

If we are having thoughts that create fear, & anxiety, asking ourselves, is this true?

If the answer contains even 1% no, let it go. Just saying to self, that's not the truth, at this moment I don't know the 100% truth about future, I choose to let it go, will loosen the hold on the fear and anxiety.

Taking pleasure in small things, and blessing it for being present in your life at this moment.

We can experience variety of thoughts, & emotions, within even half a day. Allowing them to move through, not being attached to any one particular thought and emotion, becoming present, and giving the space for joy, love, laughter, compassion to co-exist, can bring balance and harmony to our lives, no matter how the circumstances are presenting themselves at the moment.

The smallest shift will create tremendous results.

You are the shift-shapers of your life.

Shift one thing and shape your well-being, sense of self and connection to a different direction.

64

Blame is a corrosive for the soul.

The first blame that we are introduced to in Torah is Adam. Adam blamed his wife for giving him the apple to eat.

Blame, gives the power and responsibility of self to another.

Blame is another word for helpless.

As soon as we blame, we have made ourselves helpless, hopeless, and powerless.

Blame is also intertwined with feeling of guilt and shame, together it's a potion that

results in a broken self.

It took Adam 130 years to realize to say "I made a mistake", as soon as he came to that realization, he had his third child, Seth.

Once we have the realization and we take responsibility, rather than putting our life's power in someone else's hand, we give birth to new ideas, creativity in life, & deeper connection.

Run as far away as possible from blame.

Blame no one, no thing, no circumstance, and that includes the self.

Know that in your hands lies the power of choice.

Know that you are the only one who is held responsible for the choices.

Know that just because there was blame upto today, tomorrow can be a different story.

Lead an empowered life, by taking responsibility for the choices in your life, not from a place of blame of self, but from a place of having the power to choose differently today.

Today, exercise your right to choose, even if that choice is just a shift in thought process.

-65

The law of gravity would state that if you drop something in air no matter from what height, you can be sure that the object will eventually fall on earth. The time it takes depends on its mass.

There is one phenomenon on earth that defies gravity. We are so used to seeing it, that we don't think twice about it.

That is the phenomenon of a tree.

It is capable of defying the gravitational pull of earth and grow upward. Some trees like the Redwood grow extremely tall.

Life has its own gravitational pull.

The gravity of life are those events, circumstances that are bound to pull us down. They are bound to bring us to earth, the weight of situation can determine with what speed there is psychological and emotional fall.

There is one phenomenon that defies this gravity.

Just like a tree, it moves and grows upwards.

This phenomenon is called Faith.

Faith defies gravity.

It's a spiritual law.

Faith not only doesn't allow for psychological and emotional fall, but rather it propagates its growth to taller and higher states of being.

Faith is the roots of our being, it's what feeds our soul, what gives us strength to move upward, & what inspires us to go beyond ourself to bear branches that provide shade and bear fruits that provide food and sustenance to others.

Faith shows itself in many different forms and shapes.

Faith in G-d for His constant providence.

Faith that we are guided at all times and in all places.

Faith that we have been equipped with everything we need to go through circumstances and situations as they arise.

Faith in our purpose and mission, even if we are not sure what that is, we have Faith that where we find ourselves is perfect in fulfillment of Our Divine destiny.

Faith in our soul and it's light.

Faith that even though we don't understand why things happen as they happen, there is Divine plan.

Faith gives rise to resiliency and buoyancy, & gives the structure of our lives, our trunk, stability and strength.

We are made with two polar opposites.

We have the possibility of falling, being pulled down by the gravity of our lives, AND, we have the possibility of rising, growing and moving upward with circumstances of our lives.

We possess both.

We are humans, we can fall. Our fall is not lack of our faith. It's the gravitational pull of life.

However, we have a choice.

If we fall today, we can choose differently tomorrow.

If we are pulled down today, we can choose to rise up tomorrow.

We have the power of choice.

We have the inherent power of Faith.

Be the tree that you are meant to be, tall, strong, with beautiful shades and bearing delicious fruit.

-66

Break loose from the holds of the past by blessing it with love and light.

Some parts of our past can chain us, limit us, drain us, and put us in a tight rope.

Any movement in present moment and in future will be directed by this limitation.

The past is our treasure, it's our story, it's what has made us to be who we are today. However, our past can also be source of pain, regrets, and suffering.

Our past holds the power of our future only if we are able to bless every part of our past, no matter how painful it has been. It's not to forget the past, as is common in our every day language.

Not at all, every moment of our lives matters, specially the most painful ones, since within those painful moments lies the kernel of light.

We bless the past by holding those moments in a place of compassion.

We bless the past by reframing our story, and looking at it from a different facet and angle.

We bless the past by thanking it for all the ways that it has presented itself up to this moment, even the painful moments.

We bless the past by forgiveness of ourselves, of life, and of others.

We bless the past by injecting tremendous love into our past.

We would rather neglect, and abandon some parts of our past. Inject love to all parts, infuse light to all parts.

Utilize the power that lies within these moments and allow them to be the fuel that propels you forward.

In this way no part of the past holds you, chains you and keeps you in a tight rope.

Your past becomes your treasure that perpetually moves you forward.

The moments of your past hold the key to your evolvement and your elevation.

Don't throw the key out, by wanting to forget some parts of the past.

Bless every part, every moment, and inject love into every event.

It's only then that you are free to fly.

-67

*T*oday is Pesach Sheini, the second Pesach.

It came about as a result of some people complaining to Moses that due to circumstances not of their own making, they weren't able to bring the Passover offering on Pesach.

Moshe brings this up to G-d.

G-d agrees with the complaint and institutes a day, 14th of Iyar, for those who weren't able to bring the offering.

Pesach Sheini, is a day of second chances.

It's for us to internalize the gift of second chance.

Where in your life do you require a second chance?

Do you need to give yourself a second chance?

Do you need to give a relationship with another a second chance?

Do you need to give parts of your life a second chance?

Today is the day.

In our human psyche, if we have missed an opportunity, we might spend years being sorry for having missed moments of opportunities, then blaming our life for missed chances.

G-d tells us it's never too late.

Do not despair over missed opportunities.

There are opportunities around you no matter you are 20 or 80.

There are always second chances.

Give yourself the gift of second chance.

Give those parts of your life that lacks, second chance.

Give your relationships second chance.

The idea of too late doesn't exist.

Today is the day, awaken the second chance, reboot, and reconnect.

I would like to dedicate today to my beloved grandfather, Rahim Bolour, whose yartzeit is today.

He was the epitome of second chances.

Thank you Baba bozoorg.

-68

The growth chart ruler used for when kids are physically growing is easy to use. The child stands next to the ruler and marks the height. At some point the markings stop.

We never stop growing, yes physically we stop growing, however, our spiritual, mental and emotional growth continues till the day we take our last breath.

What are the markers for spiritual, mental and emotional growth?

Faith

Trust

Kindness

Compassion

Giving

Patience

Tolerance

Forgiveness

Hard to anger

Open heart

Honesty

Using words mindfully

Joyful countenance

Leading an authentic life

Having integrity

Seeing light within everything including darkness

Love of G-d, love of life, love of the journey of life, love of every soul encountered on this journey

This growth is never to be measured against others. It's only to be measured in comparison to our own chart.

When we compare, it would be like taking a child and measuring them with someone else's growth chart.

We can become aware through Torah, We can learn from Tzadikim, we can have a view of what an elevated life looks like by connecting to the patriarchs and matriarchs, we can learn how to strive for greater spiritual capacity by connecting to the sages and prophets. However, we are never to compare to anyone.

We have our unique soul, gifted to us by G-d with its unique gifts on our own unique journey.

We are all on a journey of growth.

Everything in our life should be seen through the eyes of growth.

As we go through life, and as we encounter different situations, we should always ask what does this want me to see? What aspect of myself does this want me to expand?

We are never to tell someone else who is going through a painful situation, this is for your growth. Our role is to give love, compassion, listening heart, & listening mind.

We can only and only be growth chart experts for ourselves, never for another.

Compare yourself to yourself on your journey.

Where were you 10, 5, 2, years ago?

Where were you yesterday?

Where are you today?

Where do you wish to be, only in terms of maturity of soul, 1 year from now, 5, 10, 20, 30 years from now?

If you take one aspect of soul growth to work on, it automatically feeds everything else. They all work together, they are all embedded within each other.

As we are entering into Shabbat, it's a perfect time to reflect, since on Shabbat if we are intuned, we have greater insight into our connection and spiritual well-being.

Use the opportunities of today, where you find yourself at, both the good and not so good, to grow mentally, emotionally and spiritually.

Use the moments of today to expand your capacity for soul maturity of tomorrow.

-69

The sacred feminine is
Internal

Patient

Compassionate

Nurturing

Embracing

Loving

Has the capacity to withhold from self to give to other.

Has the capacity to ignite hidden potential.

Has the capacity to heal the other.

Has the capacity to bring order to chaos.

Has the capacity to awaken serenity and calm even within the most dire situations.

Has the capacity to awaken the Divinity within with great humility and no fanfare.

Has the capacity to take different ingredients and create something greater than the sum of its parts.

Has the capacity to unite together.

Chava is the name of first female.

Chava is derivative of word Chaya, meaning the living one. It is the embodiment of essence of life and the ability to create life. Chava, the mother of all life, is not only able to procreate, but also to nourish and enhance all aspects of life.

The ability of chava, and all mothers is to be able to take something from state of potential, nurture it, and bring it into state of actual.

Today, we honor the sacred feminine, our own Chava, manifested as our selfless, patient, nurturing, loving, caring mothers.

Today, we also look at aspects of our lives and notice where it needs to be nurtured, where there needs a new life to be breathed into, where is the dormant potential waiting to become activated, & which part needs to be reshaped.

Today, we both honor and activate the sacred feminine.

Happy Mother's Day!

-70

The future that one wants to live into, is formed by the moments that one experiences and forms in the present.

In these experiences is a whole set of belief systems. The belief systems gear the possibilities towards a certain direction and it always happens in the present moment.

Yes, we are afraid of what the future holds, of the unknown and uncertainties.

When we describe a future that's of doom and gloom, guess what? We automatically, unconsciously live into a future that's doom and gloom. Since this is our experience at the moment, we extrapolate outcome that matches what's being described.

However, if we are able to be creative, and innovative with the way we describe the future, we live into that creativity. We walk into that innovation. Our whole mental state finds ways to be creative since that's what's being experienced at the present moment.

This is not about positive thinking.

It is about creating a future through our words.

This future can be formed through language that's used at the present moment, committing to it and continuously walking into it.

Using words to create a future consciously is called Generative language. Generative language is a form of action unto itself.

It allows for a possibility of a future to be born into existence.

A generative language is not a dream or hope but rather a future that you commit yourself to.

What are some of the generative and creative language that you can use today to shape your tomorrow?

What can you commit yourself to today, and continuously commit yourself to be the author of your tomorrow?

What possible future can you give birth to by using generative language that you can continuously walk into?

Use language to create possibilities.

Use commitment to walk into those possibilities.

The navigation and authorship of your life is in your language that you use in real-time.

Use it to create and generate.

-71

Fire illuminates

Fire changes the status of a thing from one state to another. An example of that would be cooking

Fire gives warmth and heat

Fire can also burn and destroy if not controlled

Today is Lag B'Omer, 33rd day of Omer, and the day of passing of Rabbi Shimon Bar Yochai. He was an Illuminator. He revealed the inner workings and dimensions of the Torah, and is the author of Zohar.

He lived at a time of one of the greatest devastations to land of Israel and the Jewish people, the destruction of second Temple. Yet, it was during this exile that he was the light and warmth that was needed to fan the flames within hearts for then and two thousand years of exile.

Today, we have access to this illumination and fire.

Fan your inner fire

Fan the fire to burn all those aspects that are no longer soul serving.

Fan the fire of love of G-d.

Fan the fire of love of life.

Fan the fire of passion, passion that's directed to your connection with G-d and your purpose in life.

Allow this inner fire to change you, transform you

Don't stop there

Fan the fire in others

Illuminate for others

Warm others hearts

Today there is revelation of inner fire, and revelation of holy fire.

We are still in exile but that doesn't mean that we can't fan the fire within.

We are in a space of confinement but that doesn't mean that we can't have passion and warmth.

Rabbi Shimon, made a clearing for us, and has given us all the tools we need to fan this holy flame, no matter where we find ourselves at.

Be the warmth, light and illumination that the world so badly needs.

Fan the flame.

-72

The only living being that can bring harmony to two opposite forces is the human being.

The human being is the only force in nature that can bring balance into contradictory forces.

Take spiritual vs physical

Holy vs mundane

Light vs dark

Finite vs infinite

The reason we can do that, we contain all within us, all at the same time.

The angels are all spiritual, animals are all physical, the hybrid between the two, is the human.

The struggle of human for thousands of years has been the struggle of bringing harmony into these opposing aspects of self and creation.

The struggle has come about as a result of either/or approach.

If I strive for spiritually then I have to abandon physicality. If I strive for light, I have to walk away from darkness, if I want to touch the infinite, I have to subdue the finite.

The only way to bring balance is to know that we are both at the same time. We need not abandon our humanity for sake of spirituality, rather we enliven our humanity with spirituality.

Light is given meaning by us, when we have walked through darkness.

We touch the infinite when through our finite physical body we do acts that invite the infinite in.

G-d desires to have a dwelling in the physical world.

It is only and only in this physical world, in the mundane, finite, existence of reality, within the actions of human beings that all forces of creation can unite together.

The human, the one who struggles, the one who can fall lower than animals, the one who can be seeped in darkness, the one who looses its way, the one who is blinded by physical forces, is the one who can also rise above the angels, transcend physical reality, enliven the abandoned, reach heights of awareness and connection.

You, the human, can bring all aspects of creation to harmony.

You, through all your contradictions is where resides all balance.

You, through all your struggles, is where G-d desires to reside.

You contain the whole universe within.

Your purpose, to harmonize.

-73

*N*oach found grace in G-d's eye.
Bereshit 6:8

The next verse goes on to say that Noach was a tzaddik and walked wholeheartedly with G-d.

How do we gain grace in G-d's eye?

By being wholesome, & wholehearted.

A wholehearted person is one who is whole with everyone.

It is one, who is complete with circumstances of life.

It is one who is aware of his/her smallness as well as his/her greatness.

It is one who is aligned to their calling and life purpose.

It is one who is whole in relationship with G-d. He stands with all of himself in the relationship, with his shortcomings as well as gifts and talents.

It is one that is not dissected in self, and their life not separated.

A wholesome person takes risk. The risk of being completely themselves, not heeding to pressures of surrounding and melding into current ideology. The risk of being authentic.

Noach, was different than the culture of his time. He stood for his values, and with great patience answered G-d's call to build the Arc.

The Arc took hundreds of years to build, everyone saw, and everyone made fun. Everyone told him, he was crazy. Everyone told him, flood? What flood? You are out of your mind.

Did he stop? NO.

A wholesome person has great courage.

The courage to have convictions in life, and to stand for them.

Are you wholesome with life, people who have been on your path, and yourself?

Do you stand with all of yourself with G-d?

Do you have the courage to stand for your soul's calling, and not be swayed by outside forces?

Noach saved the world by being wholesome and having the courage, patience and stamina to act on his calling.

You too, are a Noach in corner of your world.

G-d looks to you to uplift, elevate, and save your corner of the world.

Are you willing to take risk on yourself by being wholesome and authentic?

Do you have the courage to walk wholeheartedly with G-d and find grace in his eyes?

74

There is a safe space within that no thing, no one, no circumstance, no failure, no insult, no shame, can touch.

Get familiar with this space.

It's the part of self that perpetually dances and moves regardless of anything outside of itself.

Get to know this space.

The more aware you are of this space, the greater the ability to be nourished and nurtured by it.

It belongs to you, it's yours to enter into, it's yours to embrace.

Go there when you feel anything less than joy, harmony, balance, compassion, love.

Go there when you are in need of warmth, reassurance, and hope.

Let that space engulf you, embody you, engage you, and from here, come forth, step out into the world with confidence, and assurance that you are above it all.

Go in to come out.

This space is the quintessential self, the part of self that's always connected to G-d no matter.

It's a safe space that never defines nor limits you.

It opens the path to possibilities beyond your current limitations, whatever the limitations might be, physical, mental, emotional, monetary, social.

It's always inviting you to enter.

Are you willing to answer the invitation?

–75

The awake person always asks the question "Where am I?"

This is the first question that was asked of Adam by G-d, after he placed himself in a state of existential doubt due to partaking of the fruit of good and bad.

The answer to this simple yet profound question is the opening to the direction we are heading.

Where am I consciously?

Where am I putting my energy, thoughts?

Where am I directing my focus?

Am I in a state of blame?

If yes

Redirect

Am I in a state of complacency?

If yes

Redirect

Am I in a state of resentment?

If yes

Redirect

Am I in a state of jealousy?

If yes

Redirect

Am I in a state of no not me, no I can't, no why me?

If yes

Redirect

Am I in a state of confusion, darkness, doubt?

If yes

Redirect

Am I in a state of pain?

If yes

Have compassion for the self

Where am I?

Be honest with yourself, don't judge where you are at a particular moment. Just notice where you are and if it's anything less than your best and highest self, redirect.

Our brain has a Velcro for negative.

Negative events, negative words spoken, negative memories, negative conditioning.

It has to, it's a way of protection responding from the hind brain. It's a survival mechanism of not getting hurt.

However, that protection also stops us from fully opening our heart, from fully experiencing ourselves in the moments, from fully being available to life.

Where are you?

Is a question that G-d is asking us everyday of our lives.

To be partners with G-d, we ask ourselves the same question so we can step forth in life with our best self.

Where am I?

-76

Quantum synchronization is when two separate movements be it with object or living thing, start to attune and conform to each other's movement.

Take a pendulum of a clock for example, if you put a few clocks together and move the pendulum at different times, within a very short few minutes all the pendulums will start to move together.

Another example would be movement of school of fish, or the flight of flock of birds. They are all synchronized.

There is a force in nature that constantly looks for synchronization. It looks to harmonize together. Even though we think of nature as opposing forces, however, in actuality nature always looks to attune and cohere.

The humans are the same way, the coherence is much more subtle.

The same synchronization that happens with pendulum of clocks happens with human heart beats and brain waves of people put in the same room for sometime.

We unknowingly effect each other just by our presence.

If you enter a room and there is a very peaceful person right across you, the body picks up on that, before even you as the conscious mind picks up on it.

The heart rate and brain waves start synchronizing to the peaceful persons heart rate.

The reverse is also true, you encounter a nervous, chaotic person. Once you leave their presence you might feel drained. You become out of sync.

You can be that peaceful or chaotic person for others. Others will attune to you.

The implications of this are tremendous especially at these times of families being together in the same space for so long.

We all synchronize together.

Spouses cohere and adjust to each other's rhythm.

Children synchronize to the parents rhythm and to their siblings.

Children synchronize to parents rhythm even if they are in a different house or even far away.

Our inner balance and peace doesn't just effect us.

Our presence effects all those around us, even those who we feel a connection to but are far away.

The information that we send through our heart, and brain, gets picked up by all those around us.

You want your children peaceful, you need to set the rhythm.

You want your children loving, you need to send out those heart waves.

You want your children happy, you need to be it first.

The same is true with spouse.

You be the person that you like everybody else becoming.

Everyone will synchronize to it.

What brain waves are you putting out?

What heart energy are you exuding?

Become mindful of that, for everyone around you will synchronize to it.

-77

And G-d tested Abraham with 10 tests. Test in Hebrew is Nassah. It has the same letterings as Nes which means miracles.

Another meaning for Nes is a sign or a banner.

In Judaism when words have different meanings but have the same lettering, there is an underlying connection.

We think of test in many different ways:

G-d is testing what I'm choosing

G-d is testing how good I am

G-d is testing my abilities

G-d is testing my strength

G-d is testing my faith

G-d is testing my response

G-d is testing my wisdom

When we feel we are being tested is when we are going through a very challenging time, a great hardship, chaotic times.

A test in actuality is a banner. A banner is a sign that stands out, it's on higher ground than everything else.

When we feel we are being tested, it's an invitation to become a banner, to rise above the current capabilities and abilities, not because G-d needs to know what I am capable of, No!!

It's because I need to know what I am made up of.

G-d knows who we are in essence and what strengths we have.

It is us that needs to know in practice what faith in face of difficulty looks like, what strength in face of hardship looks like, what wisdom in face of chaos looks like.

What looks like a test, is an invitation to be a banner and a call to clear a pathway for miracles.

In scripture when it says Abraham was tested, it could be read as Abraham was raised higher. It could be interpreted as Abraham became a banner.

Abraham did become a banner for his children, us, for thousands of years.

As Abraham answered each invitation to rise higher, miracles came through him and for him.

Every time you are going through a hardship, know that if you answer the call, you are being invited to become a banner, and clear the pathway for miracles to come through.

G-d knows you clearly, your strengths, your wisdom, your essence.

Do you know yourself clearly?

Can you be the banner that G-d sees in you?

Can you be the miracle the G-d believes in you?

-78

*G*iving up superstitions that's embedded within our psyche takes awareness and practice.

A person of faith does not give power to outside forces. She/he is not afraid that some unknown force is controlling its life, some unknown energy has brought them bad luck, some negative energy has changed the direction of their destiny.

A person of faith knows there is no power but G-d.

The most powerful of all superstitions is protection from "evil eye" practices, and every culture has theirs. These superstitions can rule someone's life, instead of faith.

I can name a few:

Knocking on wood, which by the way is not a Jewish concept at all

Naming objects that so called prevent "evil eye"

Wearing objects that prevent "evil eye"

Placing objects in the house that prevent "evil eye"

And so many more...

Superstitions are a form of idol worshiping. Anything we give power to outside of G-d's dominance is idol worshipping.

The human soul has all the power within it.

The power of faith, the power of connection, the power to turn darkness to light, the power of transcendence, the power of transformation.

We, who G-d has invested all these powers within us, are to be afraid of outside forces?

We are not to fall for practices and rituals that come out of fear.

Instead we are to take all that fear and superstitions, and turn it into faith.

Where afraid of negativity, pray.

Where you want to resort to rituals for protection, say words of gratitude to G-d.

Where you want to resort to superstition, say thank you G-d for always being with you, and His light and love always guiding you.

Today is Rosh Chodesh Sivan. The power of renewal and faith is within every Rosh Chodesh but especially this month as we are preparing to receive the Torah on Thursday night.

With the power of Rosh Chodesh, combined with power of our souls, let us resolve to do away with all superstitions.

Let us resolve to not give power to any entity or any negative force and redirect everything to G-d's dominance.

Let us resolve that we will only and only through faith and prayer will rise above any negativity and with G-d's help even change the negative to positive.

Let us renew our psyche.

Do you have any superstitions?

Are you willing to let them go?

Chodesh Tov!

-79

The Tabernacle was placed at the center of the Israelites encampment for all the years they were in the desert.

The tabernacle represented the relationship of Jewish people with G-d, and G-d to the Jewish people.

It was the greatest expression of love.

Through out the 40 years in desert, not only faith and trust in G-d was deepened but there was an intimacy in relationship that was created.

The center represents the heart.

Here is the greatest lesson of all:

At the center of our lives is the heart, the relationships, the love.

Relationships take time to build and fine tune. There are many elements to building strong relationships, on top of the list being faith, trust, and love.

Even if we find ourselves in desert of life, barren from everything, it cannot stop us from building relationships, from loving, trusting, and having faith.

Even if we find ourselves stripped of everything else, we are invited to go to center and rebuild everything from a place of love.

On the one hand, we are asked to place the heart at center of our lives, on the other hand we are asked to be extremely sensitive, careful, gentle, once we are there, especially as it relates to the other.

The tabernacle was always guarded, and revered.

So too, when in relationship, any relationship, be it spouse, parent and child, friend to friend, one must enter with reverence and guard their heart.

Someone's heart is sacred space. someone's love is holy. One must always be cognizant to safeguard this holy space.

To G-d this sacred space is the center of universe, and the reason of existence.

Safeguard your relationships.

Enter the heart of others with reverence.

Know that all love is holy.

Spend everyday building a bit more faith, trust and deepening of love with the other.

Know that no matter where you find yourself, this intimacy can be acquired and it needs to be placed at the center of your life.

Know that you are on holy ground once someone has opened their heart to you.

Have you placed relationships at the center of your life?

Are you cognizant of the holy space of this center?

Are you willing to safeguard this space?

Are you willing to work on deepening the trust and faith in the relationship/s?

-80

No one can assume responsibility for the choices we make in our lives, except ourselves.

This sounds very simple, but it's not.

Many times, as we start getting to know ourselves better and delve into why we do what we do, the weight and heaviness of distorted ways of thinking and disempowered actions falls on the mother, father, family and culture.

Yes, up to the point that we realize we have taken on some habitual behavior, we can put weight on others, after that very point every choice made belongs to us solely and completely.

We inherit not only physical features but also intellectual, and emotional capabilities. However, we are never to point finger. We are to become aware and if something needs to shift in order to step into our best self, to be diligent and do it.

Our own lack of will in bringing about change causes us to fall into complacency and instead of taking responsibility for how we live our lives, we keep on running in an endless loop of others bearing responsibility for our actions.

We can be aware of our dispositions, of our personality traits, know where they come from, and shift.

The human being is about growth, is about leaping the rungs of consciousness, is about moving towards an empowered self.

We are to take note both out of curiosity and a willingness to see ourselves better, but never as an excuse for staying in a certain paradigm.

Set the intention to accept responsibility for all of you, your emotional dispositions, the lens through which you see the world and life, your personality traits.

If there are parts of you that require polishing, then take action.

If there are parts of you that no longer serve your highest state of being, then shift.

Always, and always take responsibility for how you present yourself to yourself and the world. It's only from that place of responsibility that you have the power to grow.

Authentic power is when you take 100% responsibility for who you are.

Are you in your authentic power?

If yes, fantastic.

If no, then what are you willing to do to shift?

-81

H-Shem could have given us the Torah anywhere, yet He choose a lowly mountain in middle of a desert.

Adam was born in garden of Eden in middle of orchards. He eventually had to leave the garden since his consciousness fell to a point where he couldn't sustain being in the garden.

Since then, Adam's children and all subsequent generations have consciously or unconsciously wanted to find a way back to Eden. It is a faint memory within the psyche of human that being in garden is possible. That there is a utopia to aim for, a place where there is beauty, joy, unconditional love, compassion, kindness, peace, and harmony. That in this place is the secret of fountain of youth and immortality.

Since then, Adam's children have toiled, toiled emotionally with inner conflicting feelings of being, toiled psychologically with struggles of duality, toiled physically with working the land, toiled spiritually with being connected to H-Shem.

Then comes some 2,500 years later after Adam having left the garden, H-Shem chooses a group of people, the Israelites, and says I give you everything you need to find your way back to the garden. I give you the Torah. I give you myself through the Torah. I give you relationship with me.

However, this time I need you to become partners with me in reinventing the garden.

This time, with all that I'm giving you, I need you to turn the barren desert into an orchard. I give you what you need, now, I depend on you to turn the earth into a Garden of Eden, into a place of peace, harmony, oneness, love, compassion.

It's upto you to find immortality through acts of loving kindness and planting seeds of light wherever you go.

I depend on you to bring heaven to earth, because that's exactly where I want to dwell.

And G-d, choose a lowly mountain to show that yes we need to climb but not so steep that we would never make it. We need to climb spiritually, we need to make an effort.

He choose a desert, so that we can turn it into an orchard, with the gift of Torah.

We are partners with G-d, not subjects. We are co-creators of a world that is both in G-d's dream and our dream, a state of being called Garden of Eden.

He has given us the tools, the way to connect, the highest way of being. It's up to us individually and collectively to use all the gifts we have been given.

It's up to us to turn our corner of world that we find ourselves in, into a Garden.

It's up to us to turn the barren desert into an orchard, planting seeds of love, compassion, joy, kindness into our space.

Are you willing to do what it takes to make your deserted space into Garden of Eden?

Are you willing to be in partnership with G-d to make a dream a reality?

-82

On Shavout, G-d is telling us "I love you, and I want to be in relationship with you", and us saying "yes".

The greatest event that changed the consciousness of the world from there forth, was and is the revelation of H-Shem on mount Sinai to a group of slaves who had left Egypt some 50 days earlier, and now attained the highest level of Being.

The Israelites having moved from one end of spectrum of being bound and enslaved, to another spectrum of love and freedom.

It is in this state of being that the Jewish people received the Torah and were able to come into partnership with the Master of Universe.

This partnership has many facets.

It's the ability of opposite forces uniting,

mundane and sacred, spiritual and material.

On Shavout the world became one unified expression of Divinity.

G-d gave us the power to inject love into every aspect of existence.

He gave us the possibility of infusing the coarseness of physical world with the beauty and light of the spiritual world.

On Shavout we reach the highest level of our being, the ability to enter the 50th gate of understanding.

G-d himself takes us to this gate, and for a moment He allows us to know with every cell of our body, with all levels of consciousness, with all levels of self, what it means to be our fullest potential.

Tonight we get a glimpse of our deepest relationship with G-d and what's possible.

Tonight, we enter into the greatest state of love, love of G-d, love of others, love of our soul and mission.

The Torah can not be received in any other state but love.

The partnership can not be made in any other state but unity.

To enter the 50th gate we must have left behind all those aspects of self that limit us and bind us.

We must have left behind the consciousness of not possible, to, with G-d all is possible.

We must have left behind our separations, in whatever shape or form it might have showed itself.

We must have left behind complacency, and indifference to the world around us.

Tonight G-d is saying "I love you and I want to be in partnership with you".

Are you spiritually ready to say "yes"?

Is your heart full of love?

Do you have a unity consciousness?

Have you left behind your limitations?

The same events that took place some 3,332 years ago at the foot of mount Sinai, take place tonight.

Will you be present to say "yes"?

Chag sameach!

83

*L*ife is unpredictable, from one moment to next dynamics can change drastically.

However, what can be predictable is the love and music of soul shared, if we choose.

This is our gift to the universe:

To lead our lives with this predictability,

To sing our song no matter the instruments we are handed.

To dance our dance, no matter the music being played.

To stand on highest ground, no matter if we are being pulled down continuously.

To express love, no matter if everything outside of us is telling us to close our hearts.

To have compassion, no matter if mass consciousness pulls us into anger.

Mass consciousness can have tremendous impact on personal consciousness. If mass consciousness is feeling anxious, afraid, reactive, and angry, it can effect our consciousness.

We can choose differently.

In this choice we are free.

Be predictable for yourself,

Choose the highest path at every juncture.

Choose to dance your particular dance, regardless.

Choose to sing your unique song, regardless.

Don't allow your unique expression be dimmed by outside mass consciousness of fear and anger.

The world needs your soul's unique song now more than ever.

Choose to be predictable to your highest expression.

What do you choose?

Do you choose the predictability of your soul's expression,

Or

the unpredictability of mass consciousness?

-84

The Israelites, a year after having received the 10 commandments in the desert, were poised to enter land of Israel.

Before the whole nation enters, Moshe Rabbeinu sends 12 elite men, one of each tribe, to scout the land and bring back report of how to best enter the land.

They came back 40 days later, and report that the land is prosperous with huge grapes and pomegranates, olives and dates, "BUT, there are giants in the land, and we are like grasshoppers in their eye".

The whole nation starts mourning at that point, crying in their own tents, feeling despondent and beaten, thinking that they left Egypt for no reason. How are they going to enter the land?

A nation that was on the highest level of spiritual status the day before, fell to the lowest level of being, just by a few words.

The words, "but we are like grasshoppers in their eyes."

That generation never made it to land of Israel.

Here is the greatest lesson of all:

When we start bringing ourselves down, when we analyze a situation and say, it looks good but I'm too small,

when we see ourselves as incapable,

When we feel incompetent,

When we feel there are giants in the world, be it any situation we find ourselves in including the current situation,

when we feel helpless,

when we feel powerless,

we loose our way. We loose our focus. We loose our ability to impact. We loose the ability to come up with a solution.

Even if we are poised to enter our highest destiny, guided by G-d, given all powers and protection, when we say "but", we give it all up. G-d can't help us at that juncture, because until we don't believe we are capable, we can't do anything, even if we are gifted with everything.

Notice the conversations you have with yourself.

Notice where you see yourself as a grasshopper.

Notice where you want to do something, however, the word "but" stops you.

Notice where you feel powerless, there is a "but" somewhere in the psyche.

Notice where you feel despondent, there is a "but" somewhere in self conversation.

Whatever situation we find ourselves in, be it personal or global, it means that we can impact, change, improve, elevate, the situation.

That won't happen unless we remove the word "but"

And

stop seeing ourselves as tiny grasshoppers.

Notice, and change the conversation.

Once the conversation changes, once you believe, all the protection and assistance you need will pour in for you from G-d.

Are you willing to change your conversations?

Are you willing to remove the word "but"?

Are you willing to no longer see yourself as a grasshopper no matter what the situation?

-85

Darkness is confusion
When life's meaning seems inscrutable, when our purpose is obscured, when our struggles seem meaningless, when our vision is confused, that's darkness.

How do you transform darkness to light?

Be a soul afire.

How?

Be a beacon of light in chaos.

Be a voice of kindness in anger.

Be a space of compassion in turmoil.

Be a heart of Faith in uncertainty.

Be with purpose in confusion.

Within every darkness there is a kernel of light.

Within every challenge there is a kernel of change.

The kernel of light waits for you to extract it.

The kernel of change waits for you to plant it.

At times like these where there is great sense of chaos and confusion,

be a soul afire.

Maybe just maybe that's why you are here right now at this moment, your soul's fire necessary to transform darkness to light.

Be a soul afire.

-86

H2O....the formula of water

H2O2.....the formula of Hydrogen Peroxide

O2.........the formula of Oxygen

H2.........the formula of Hydrogen

One atom difference within the combination of molecular structure and you have a completely different molecule.

The difference between hydrogen peroxide and water is just one atom of oxygen.

The difference between water and hydrogen is just one atom of oxygen.

Each atom combination contributes to what the molecule will become, a lack or addition of just one atom will result to completely something else.

This is also true of who we are:

Each ingredient in our lives contributes to the totality of who were are,

Our past

Our experiences

Our heritage

Our parents

Our community

Our families

Our personality

Our look

Our temperaments

You add or subtract one element and you get somebody else.

G-d made you, and desires you.

G-d desires you with your personality, your moods, your looks, your past, your experiences to make choices that elevate everything around it including itself.

The first choice is the choice of embracing the self, in all of its facets, in all of its weaknesses and strengths, in all of its confusion and clarity, in all of its doubt and knowingness.

The second choice is the choice of elevating those aspects that belittle you, disempower you, disengage you.

You cannot elevate until you don't embrace.

Not to embrace all aspects of self is like thinking that we are a different formula.

You will not be able to engage in your life and in the world fully, with only some aspects of yourself.

You are the totality of ALL your parts.

First embrace,

then integrate and

then elevate.

Are there aspects of self that have been denied?

Are there aspects of personality you would rather not have?

Are there aspects of your history you would rather change?

Are you willing to embrace and integrate?

-87

The first iconoclast in history lived some 4,000 years ago.

His name, Abraham Avinu.

An iconoclast is someone who goes against social norm, breaks the icons of society, is an outside of the box thinker, questions settled beliefs and ideas.

Abraham Avinu did exactly that, he broke the idols of his time, went against social norm, questioned everything that his surrounding told him to be or not to be.

Abraham Avinu, had many followers in his life time. How did he manage to have so many people follow him, embrace his ideas of G-dliness, abandon their belief system?

With just one attribute and one attribute only,

Kindness

He changed the world forever, by his attribute of kindness.

This has many implications for us as his direct descendants.

We are to always break the idols of our times. We are to question social norm, however, we must always do it with kindness.

We can both individually and collectively stand for change of those ideas that don't express our highest humanity, and yet do it with kindness.

We are to be iconoclasts.

We are to change and elevate the world around us, after all that's our purpose for being here, however, we are to do it with kindness that stems from G-dliness.

At times like these where there is great mayhem and confusion,

be an agent of change and yet,

be kind, be kinder and be kindest.

At times of change, be the norm breaker and yet,

Be kind, be kinder and be kindest.

Question, change, elevate, and be kind, very kind, beyond your nature kind.

-88

*Y*ou have been handed a white canvas for today.

Now paint in it.

Choose to paint wisely, for this is the last time you will be handed this combination of colors.

Tomorrow, different size canvas, different combination of colors.

This is life.

Everyday we are given different opportunities to love, to forgive, to connect, to have compassion, to listen to someone deeply, to let the people in our lives know we love them, for

This day will NEVER come again.

This day has its own unique colors.

Never again will you be handed these colors.

The expression is you have to enjoy life fully, because you never know what tomorrow brings.

The enjoyment is knowing that for today, You have connected fully

You have left no room for regrets

You have left no room for blame

You have used yourself up fully to be present for all those around you

You have used yourself up fully to love deeply and to show it.

To enjoy life fully, means that you have connected to the joy of life, to have fulfilled the fullest expression of your soul for this day, with all circumstances that has been handed to you.

Choose what you paint wisely, for this combination of colors will never be handed to you again.

-89

$\mathcal{S}$ix life lessons from centenarians:

1. Healthy mindset, to know that life has many facets, some are in form of obstacles, some in shape of challenges and pain, some in form of loss, some in form of joy and celebration, some in form of success. A healthy mind set is to know that change is inevitable and be able to adapt to change. It's to know that the only thing that doesn't change is change itself.

2. Spiritual practice on regular basis. To have faith. To know that we can't comprehend and fathom the workings of G-d. However, everything that he does has purpose. Faith allows us to rest in embrace of G-d especially at times of calamity, challenge and tragedy and know that G-d in His infinite wisdom knows how this tapestry of life needs to be woven. Part of spiritual practice is the

ability to surrender to those events that have already happened. Faith, surrender, trust, prayer, talking to G-d on regular basis are all part of spiritual practice.

3. Be around family and loved ones. We don't necessarily need proof that relationships, especially those of family and healthy friendships, add much to a person's life, both in quality and quantity. However, research has shown this very fact, that we need each other to not only to survive but to thrive. The events of past months has also shown us the importance of family and those closest to us.

4. Appreciation of life and gratefulness. To be able to see the gifts in our lives from the tiniest things that we call tiny, to the grandest, that we call grand. To be able to be grateful for all the blessings that we have been given in our life, and thank H-Shem for them. Appreciation refocuses the brain from one perspective to another and has the ability to shift our future outlook in life.

5. Living a life that has meaning and purpose to you. That meaning must be given by yourself through your talents,

your love, your connections. I hear so many times moms saying, I'm nothing just a mom. There is much meaning and purpose to that. However, must come from you. Part of the purpose is using your soul's light to serve and be of service. This can come in many shapes and forms. You decide.

6. Last but not least, exercise, movement and ofcourse nutrition.

Life is in G-d's hand. However, as partners with him in life, there is much we can do to be healthy and happy centenarians. We have put much emphasis on diet and exercise and they are very important, however, that's not the whole picture, nor is it the whole formula. At the same time that we exercise our body, we must exercise our brain muscles, to be able to refocus, reshape our perception.

We must nurture our soul, to have spiritual practice so that our faith is strengthened, our trust in G-d is established, and the ability to surrender to life events that's beyond our control.

We must be able to allow the light of soul to shine through, so we have lived a life of purpose and meaning.

We must nurture our connection to our loved ones, and continue reconnecting with greater depth and love.

We must nurture our ability to appreciate, be grateful, and see good in everything and everyone.

If you are doing all above, excellent, if not, where do you need to make adjustments?

When are you going to start the adjustments?

-90

"See, I have placed before you today the life and the good, death and evil. Choose life."

These are some of last words of Moshe Rabbeinu before he passes away and a few months before the Israelites are poised to enter the land of Israel.

The question is why does Moshe asks us to choose life, isn't that obvious that we would choose life?

The answer is not a simple yes or no, since we have many dynamics at play.

Choosing life is a conscious choice and Moshe is asking us the be aware and choose consciously.

When we fall into our impulses, and act within the context of our personalities we are in danger of not choosing life. We are choosing unconsciously.

Some examples would be:

The times when we don't choose consciously and hurt another,

The times when we don't choose consciously and speak bad about one another,

The times when we don't choose consciously and continue to hold a grudge,

The times when we don't choose consciously and start blaming rather than taking responsibility,

The times we don't choose consciously and don't forgive,

The times when we don't choose consciously not using our faith to stand in darkness but rather seep into it deeper and deeper,

The times when we don't choose consciously and we forget to appreciate G-d for all the blessings he has bestowed upon us,

The times when we don't choose consciously and we fall in doubt, & chaos,

The times when we don't choose consciously and worry.

Every time we don't choose consciously and we hurt, blame, speak bad, and the likes, we have chosen evil and death. Not death as dying of physical body, but death as obscuring the G-dly and the goodly.

Every time we obscure and cover up the light with our actions, we are also effecting the rest of the world.

The world becomes just a bit darker, just a bit less goodly. All because I didn't choose consciously.

Every time we choose consciously and go beyond our impulses, go beyond our personalities, go beyond our calculations of right and wrong, we have chosen to remove the veil of darkness, just a tiny bit, and reveal more light into the world.

Moshe is asking us be conscious of our actions with everything we do, with all our interactions, with all our connections, to bring G-dliness and goodness into every moment.

Choose life.

-91

The birds awaken the dawn.

The birds start singing right before the light of sun. If you pay attention, it starts from one or two birds and soon you have a variety of tunes being sung by different birds.

They are called the dawn chorus.

It was thought that birds start singing at such an early hour to attract mate, the stronger they sing, the wider their voice goes, and their ability to attract a mate is enhanced. That is true but that's not all.

Science has shown that their singing has much greater implications than just mate attraction.

The dawn chorus actually awakens the earth to the morning.

The bird song creates a chain reaction in the soil, creating an effect on plant leaves, on earthworms, soil and nutrients in the soil, to promote growth.

The bird song creates a vibrational shift on earth every morning that awakens the earth itself.

It has been shown that in those areas that the birds sing, the plants are healthier, greener, the trees stronger.

Here is a profound lesson for us:

The birds have no idea what the day brings them, where their food comes from, how far they need to travel to find food, if they will attract a mate or not, but one thing they know for sure, that they need to sing.

They sing and awaken the dawn.

They sing and awaken the earth.

They sing and bring vibrational shift.

We too, can awaken the dawn. Just like birds, we don't have to know the details of our life, we can trust that all will be provided for, the food, the security, the mate, our job is to sing, to sing praises to G-d.

Our singing causes a vibrational shift within our home and within our environment. The shift allows for nutrients to be awakened in us to promote growth.

What are those nutrients?

Faith

Trust

Surrender

Love

Compassion

Peace

Balance

Serenity

Imagine waking up everyday, and rather than remembering all the events that happened yesterday, all the worries, not wanting to deal with problems, not wanting to face the challenges, complaining about another day, you sing.

Imagine that's the first thing you do.

Imagine you awaken your consciousness with songs of praise.

Imagine you awaken your body with songs of trust.

Imagine you awaken your home with songs of love.

Imagine the vibrational shift you would bring to your home.

Imagine the nourishment you bring to your soul and all those around you.

Wake up dreading, dragging, complaining
Or
Wake up singing?
The choice is yours.

-92

Is life about the journey,
Or

Is life about the destination,

Or

Both?

Four out of five books of Torah is about Moshe Rabbeinu, his birth, his death, and everything else in between. The everything else in between consists of him taking the Jewish people out of slavery, be the channel of G-d's miracles, be the receiver of 10 commandments and Torah from G-d, be the giver of 10 commandments and Torah to Jewish nation, be the only person in history of Judaism to speak to G-d directly, be the one who leads the Jewish people through desert for 40 years, be the one who changed the Israelites from a tribe into a nation, and yet he never made his destination, the land of Israel.

Everything that's written and everything that's been passed down to us, became to be while he and the Israelites, were on their journey.

The 10 commandments given while on their journey,

The 13 Divine attributes that G-d communicated to Moshe, while they were on their journey,

The tabernacle was made while on their journey,

The miracle of manna was experienced for 38 years while on their journey,

The Israelites became highly organized as a nation, each knowing their place of encampment and their contributions while on their journey,

The Kohanim came to be the priests and high priests while on their journey,

The Torah, all its teachings, everything we are today as Jews, came to be while on their journey.

Profound lesson here:

Don't ever put out anything for later, it's the journey that makes us who we are.

It's the journey that gives us the depth, the perceptions, the fulfillment's, the joys, through traveling the struggles, the unknowns, the chaos, and the challenges.

It's important to have a destination, to have a goal and move towards it, however, it's who we become through reaching our destination that matters.

It's what we put out while on our journey towards self-realization that makes us who we are.

It is the moment to moment interactions, with life, with oneself, with G-d, with each other that shapes our character and gives meaning to our name.

The moments, days, and weeks of quarantine have been referred to as "life on pause".

We are never on pause.

We are in different dynamics, but not on pause.

We are in moments of our journey, not on pause.

Every moment is a moment added to our journey.

It's important to have a vision, goal, destination, and continuously step into it. However, it's about what we become through the journey of our life, through the steps we take to reach the destination, through closing the gap between destination and where you find yourself at, that makes the connections and brings out the gifts of the soul.

Is life about the journey, destination, or both?

You decide.

-93

The way out is the way through

Often times when we are in situations that are painful, chaotic, and we find ourselves fragmented and splintered, we want to change the mood, or change the environment we find ourselves in.

Everything, every event, every situation that we are faced with, everyday of our lives, gets recorded in our system, and until is not processed it will never leave the system.

Through out the ages we have invented amazing escape mechanisms, alcohol, drugs, frivolous time spending, procrastination, excessive eating, excessive exercise, TV binging, excessive sports following, gossiping, anger, being shy, being a control freak, excessive socializing, thinking that we have no time, feeling of overwhelm. All of the above are ways to not deal with our inner pain.

Whether the pain happened at 3, or 30, it's irrelevant, to the body and psyche is all the same. It acts as if it happened now, in the present. The pain becomes the undercurrent, the hum, the vibrational tone, through which we lead our lives, and we might not ever know. We might consider ourselves as someone who has life by the leash and can turn its head any which way, yet if there are situations, pains that haven't been processed, unknowingly the pain is what's holding the leash.

Our situations, challenges, pain, chaos, fragmentation, sadness, must all first be honored and acknowledged.

No situation, no pain will ever be healed by turning the other way, somewhere, someday, it will show its head.

The pain, the fragmentation, the sadness, the scatteredness in and of itself is not bad, it's a set of information, it's what we do with it, how we process it, how we disregard, or discard of it, that could become problematic.

We often times feel if we acknowledge our pain, we will drown in it. The reverse is true, if we don't acknowledge, we will drown in habits of avoidance, and our true, authentic self will be hidden underneath all the hiding.

Acknowledgment is the first step.

Honoring is the second step.

Holding the pain, conflict, struggle, and everything alike is a space of self-compassion is the third step.

Injecting light into those spaces is the fourth step. We inject light by faith, trust, knowing that no matter what the situation looks like, we are held in G-d's arms, understanding that we are on our soul journey, knowing that everything in our life is aligned to our purpose and mission.

Do you have any habits that might indicate you are running away from something within yourself?

Are you willing to acknowledge them?

Remember:

The way out is the way through.

-94

Nowhere
What did you read the above as?

Nowhere could be read two ways:

No where

Now here

Both is absolutely correct. It depends on state of your mind, and the way it perceives things.

No where, is a perception that one is lost, or something is missing.

Now here, is a perception that one is present, available to the moment.

Two different perceptions that stand completely opposite of each other, one is absent or missing, the other is present and available.

This is a very small example of how our brain picks up information according to the state of mind it finds itself in.

When we are happy, the sensory information that's picked up from our surroundings is completely different than when we are in a solemn state of mind.

Our perception is directly linked to our state of mind. Our actions are dependent on our perceptions. We pick up a set of information from outside and we act on it. Action could be a form of speech as well.

If we take the above example, we will act completely differently if we feel lost vs, if we feel present.

Our state of mind is determined by many factors, however, we are not at its mercy.

We can consciously train our state of mind and actively change our perception.

We can consciously seek for the good in everything we see.

We can consciously seek for the good in circumstances and situations.

We can consciously seek good in other people.

We can consciously seek good in our past, present and future.

We can train ourselves to pick up information that's beneficial to our well being, growth, and evolvement.

Both sets of information are true. It's not to say one doesn't exist, both exists at the same time. Both has the potential to become our reality.

Choose the sets of information that you are receiving every moment consciously.

It has the potential of redirecting your emotions and recalibrating your actions.

Always ask can I see where I find myself at differently? Is there information here that I'm not seeing and seeking?

No where

Or

Now here

Both true, both real.

If you perceived no where, you can consciously choose now here.

You can always consciously shift what you perceive.

You choose.

-95

*T*he salmon journeys every 5-7 years to a place where it was laid as egg.

Salmons have an acute sense of smell, assisting them to find their way home, upstream to where they were laid as eggs and were hatched.

Through their sense of smell they are able to find the stream of water that they traveled downstream some 7 years before, this time traveling upstream with one intention only, to lay their eggs.

They are extremely determined and even jump 10 ft waterfalls to reach their destination. They have an extraordinary drive to reach home, and have to pass through many predators before getting there. Once they arrive, they lay eggs and die. The cycle repeats itself in 5-7 years.

There are profound lessons from the salmon:

The sense of smell in Judaism is associated with the soul. It's the ability to be connected to our internal self, to the light within.

The Salmon follows the smell in the water to find its way home, and nothing stands in its way.

In our journey of life, being connected to our soul, allows us to navigate life through the predators of life — the predators being worry, sadness, fear, gives us the capacity to jump 10 ft waterfalls upstream, allows us to go against the current of present time, not falling into doubt and anxiety of general population.

Being connected to our soul, allows us to get connected to our purpose and mission, becoming determined, focused, and have extraordinary drive in life to reach the place where we can lay our eggs. The eggs here, represent those imprints, elevations, good deeds that we leave here on earth.

It's also, the value of returning to our essence, moving upstream through emotional waters to rebirth spiritual knowledge and insight.

Being connected to our soul, gives us the power to move against the odds, with energy, focus, and no obstacle standing in our way.

When we find ourselves lost, incapable, despondent, and can't navigate our way through life, we can harness our strength by connecting to our internal light.

Let that be our guidance system.

Let that be our navigational tool.

Let that be the power beyond all movements.

Let that be the focus of our lives.

This way we will never be lost, no matter what's in front of us. It will always guide us home, to a place where we can give birth to the newness of self.

Do you navigate life by being connected to your soul?

If yes, great, Strengthen the connection.

If not, what steps can you take to do so?

-96

G-d created the universe, and deeply desires to be "seen" in every aspect of creation.

G-d, the infinite, the all knower, the all giver, the creator of all things, the king of universe, desires to be "seen" by the finite, paradoxical, human being.

This act of being "seen" is innate in the human being, who is the microcosm of the whole universe.

Every human being deeply desires to "be seen".

This desire starts with child to parent, expands in later years to a spouse, and close friends.

The human being grows spiritually, mentally and emotionally in an environment where they are "seen", deeply "seen".

What does it mean to be seen?

It's when you are acknowledged.

It's when your inner feelings and inner conflict is acknowledged.

It's when a safe space is created for the other to be and express.

It's when there is no judgement on how the person is feeling and thinking.

It's when you are fully present for the other, meaning that you are actively engaged with them, without watching TV, being on the phone, or the computer.

Children are especially sensitive to this, and when they feel they were not "seen" problems can arise in later years.

To "see" a child, it doesn't mean having them signed up for 10 different classes, going on 8 vacations a year, and giving them everything they ask for.

No.

It means to be present with them.

It means that their feelings are acknowledged rather than discounted.

It means that they are validated as individuals and not as performers of getting A and A plus in school.

It means their importance is validated no matter what they choose as profession in their lives.

It means that your love for them is anchored and shown, especially at times when they show weakness.

How many times have children expressed their frustration and we have discounted them by saying, "you think you have it bad, look at....."

To "be seen" is the greatest act of love.

Do you "see" your children?

Is there a safe space for them to express their conflicts, hurts, pain, worry, anxiety?

Are they validated for who they are at the moment, rather than discounted?

Are you able to show them their importance to you no matter their level of performance?

Do you "see" your spouse?

And most importantly

Do you "see" yourself?

As we grow consciously and in our awareness, we must be able to hold a safe space for ourselves with great care and compassion for all those places within that we would rather not have.

An aware person is one who has been able to transfer the need to be seen by parent, spouse, or someone close, to the self.

Actively being present, actively listening, actively loving, are all parts of being "seen".

G-d desires to be "seen".

We, innately desire to be "seen".

Give the greatest gift you possibly can to G-d, to your children, your spouse, your friends, and importantly to yourself, by "seeing".

"See".

-97

*I*ndividual cells in our body have a finite life span, and when they die off, they are replaced by new ones.

There are between 50-75 trillion cells in our body, each type of cell having its own life span. Red blood cells live on average 4 months, white blood cells about a year, skin cells two to three weeks.

It is said that every 7-10 years we essentially become new person since in that time most of our cells have been replaced by new ones.

Often times, we have a certain image of self that imprisons us to the image.

Our physical body is continuously changing, the cells are continuously replaced by new ones. This process is unconscious, the cells are replenished according to their own clock, regardless if we know or don't know.

If this is true of our physical body, how much more so of our spiritual, emotional and mental bodies.

How often are our spiritual, emotional and mental bodies replenished?

That's really up to us.

We have a choice in this.

From age 0-7, all information is absorbed, and our emotional, mental tendencies are all formed at those formative years.

Are we stuck to those tendencies forever?

Yes and no.

Yes, if we are at it's mercy and live life as if that's the final word.

No, if we are conscious and aware, and know that emotional, mental, and spiritual bodies are all there to be changed and formed by the conscious mind.

We are not stuck to a certain way that we defined ourself as 10 years ago, 5 years ago and even yesterday.

We have the greatest power of all, the power of choice combined with power of our awareness, to change and reshape our emotional, mental, spiritual bodies.

Do you have certain emotional tendencies?

If they are good, perfect.

If not, you are not stuck with it. It's changeable.

Do you have certain mental tendencies?

You don't have to be defined by it, it's changeable.

Do you have certain spiritual inclination?

It can expand, and contain greater levels of faith and trust.

We are always changing in all our bodies.

It does it automatically, if unconscious, it replenishes from all old set of information, if conscious, it creates from the new set of information.

Essentially we are never bound to a certain image, we can define and redefine ourselves continuously according to the growth of our awareness.

We can, if we wish, renew and replenish ourselves daily.

What set of information do you feed your spiritual, mental, emotional bodies?

Is it based on an old paradigm and image of self?

Or

Is it based on a new expanded, conscious image of self?

The choice is yours.

-98

Anything that increases separation within a person, diminishes the strength of the soul.

There are certain behaviors that cause separation. These behaviors are inauthentic to the power of the soul, and distort its ability.

These behaviors are:

- jealousy
- hatred
- non-forgiveness
- lying and being lied to, this includes all forms of cheating whether in business, and/or relationships
- anger
- despondency
- murder, which could be in form of shaming someone in public
- doubt
- fear, includes all forms of fear whether validated or not
- gossip

If we have anyone of these character traits, it means there is a part of our personality that needs healing.

The first step towards healing is awareness.

Awareness is to be able to be radically honest with self, that there are aspects within the personality that have caused separation within itself, and hence the soul and its powers.

To heal means to be whole.

Healing means that all parts of self, become integrated through love, trust, and forgiveness.

It means the person who lies, stops lying, and the person who cheats, stops cheating.

It means the person who becomes angry, looks into root cause of their pain, and works towards healing their anger.

It means that jealousy will no longer have any form of existence in psyche.

It means that fear, and doubt are actively and continuously being diminished by faith and trust.

Wholeness within our personalities allows the power of soul to come forth.

It allows for evolvement of self into higher levels of consciousness.

It allows for light of the soul to shine through.

This is our goal, to reach a place where the beauty, power, knowledge, wisdom, will, of our soul is guiding our thoughts, speech and action. Then we are no longer guided by our split personality that competes for everything, from power to love.

Are there behaviors that diminish the strength of your soul?

Can you be radically honest with self, and pick up even the minutest traces of behaviors that has separated you from your soul power?

Are you willing to become whole?

Are you willing to allow the light of your soul to be your guiding compass?

-99

*J*ust as there are seasons in nature, we humans also go through seasons of our own, not only physically but also spiritually.

Understanding that spiritually we go through seasons, is important in how we approach the changes that take place.

Each individual has their own spiritual season, and their own unique timing.

To the naked eye, it would seem that winter is completely separate than summer, however, any mature individual knows that it's a flow. It's a flow of cycles of life, and flow of cycles of growth and rebirth.

Winter is always always followed by spring. We have some winters that are harsher than others, some winters that take longer than others, however, spring always follows winter, no matter how harsh the winter has been.

There are times in our cycles of spiritual journey that we go through winter of spiritually, where it feels cold, dark, lonely, uninviting, unapproachable, nothing seems to blossom or grow no matter how much effort we are putting in.

These are times that we are being invited to hibernate, so we can recharge, and reevaluate.

When in spiritual winter the most important tool we can have is non-resistance.

Imagine the trees resisting going into winter.

Imagine animals resisting going into hibernation.

Imagine the land itself resisting becoming barren, and frozen.

Rather than resist, animals prepare.

Rather than resist, plant roots prepare.

Being in spiritual winter, takes patience and trust. Patience, in that this is exactly where I need to be at present moment to regroup and Trust that spring always follows.

There are times we go from summer of our cycle to fall. Those are times when we are being invited to shed the leaves of the old, shedding old patterns of beliefs and ideas. This doesn't happen overnight, but rather is a process and takes time.

In fall, we also start planting seeds, so we can see them grow in spring and summer.

We are always guided by G-d and the blueprint for our higher destiny into the seasons of our lives. We will go into our seasons regardless of what we think. However, how we prepare, how we utilize, how we flow through it, is completely up to us. The length of time that it takes to stay in each season is also partially up to us.

If we don't do what we are supposed to do in winter, we might stay there for a long time until we are ready to blossom and give birth to new ideas.

If we are fully stuck in newness of spring, it's going to take a long time to move into fullness of summer and enjoy the fruits of our lives.

As King Solomon says in Kohelet:

Everything has its season:

A time to sow, and a time to reap

A time to keep, and a time to discard

Understanding the season we are in, gives us tools and awareness we need to go through our seasons with great ease, non- resistance, surrender, and trust, so we can flow, grow, and become that which is our highest destiny.

Can you recognize what season you are in now?

Can you recognize what is required of you in this season, so you can effortlessly flow?

-100

Today we celebrate and honor the masculine. There are two forces within creation, masculine and feminine. Everything in this world has either of the two qualities.

The harmony and balance between the two energies brings peace, growth, and the ability to build with great love and strength.

The masculine energy in Jewish thought is the spark of creativity, wisdom, all giving, confident, and protective.

The masculine is the giver, and therefore has the ability of expansion.

The masculine is compared to the sun, it always gives heat, light and illumination.

The sun being the prime ingredient for growth and life.

It's the aspect of wisdom, inspiration, and aspiration.

The masculine because of its wisdom, is confident, knows what steps need to be taken in order to reach the destination.

It's focused and determined, with very little getting in its way. It's able to remove obstacles as they come along, always focused on where it needs to go. No confusion or lack of direction blinds the masculine.

There is always motivation, energy, and the ability to move mountains.

It's protective and shields all those he loves.

The aligned masculine is righteous, it does what is right and true, even if it means more hardship for himself. It's able to go into the world and fight for what is right, good and virtuous.

We honor the fathers today who are the manifestations of the masculine force of creation.

The strength, rock, shields, illuminators, source of life, protective forces, source of wisdom and inspiration, bearing the burden with laser sharp focus with no obstacles too big to overcome.

Happy Father's Day!

–101

Jacob was left alone and an Angel wrestled with him until break of dawn.

Then the Angel says "let me go, for dawn has broken"

Jacob says," I will not let you go unless you bless me"

Angel says to Jacob"what is your name?"

He replied, "Jacob"

The Angel says, "No longer will it be said that your name is Jacob, but Israel, for you have striven with the Divine and have overcome". Bereishit 32/25-32/29

Jacob's battle with the Angel, is man's struggle with life, it's challenges, it's ups and downs. It's also the struggle with our own self, with parts of ourselves that wants, needs, its own darker side.

This struggle happens in darkness, when we are confused, tired, hesitant and uncertain.

Once dawn breaks, the dark has no longer any power, no matter how much it has struggled it has to leave. Dawn is when light is introduced to our lives, when there is wisdom, clarity, faith. The darkness, which itself is part of Divine mission, has no choice but to leave.

We have two choices in life, either be defeated by the struggles and challenges of our lives or be blessed by them.

Jacob asks for blessing before the Angel who struggled with him leaves. He becomes Israel.

We are all called Israel because of this blessing.

When we ask for blessing from the struggles, we too become Israel.

Israel means the perpetual soldier of G-d.

Israel is one who is never stagnant, but perpetually moves, creates, and brings Divinity into all aspects of life. Israel is one who is a soldier of light, goodness, wisdom.

We become elevated, we become a force of light and goodness, not only for ourselves but for others.

Asking to be blessed by our struggles is not an easy task. We all dream of the day when we are struggle free and we no longer have to battle either outside circumstances or internal darkness.

However, we become Israel because of the struggles.

We become a force because of our agony.

We become a source of light because, not only we don't run away but we stay, wrestle, prevail and bless.

We can remain Jacob, or we can become Israel.

Are you wrestling with your challenges?

Can you ask to be blessed by your struggles?

Can you ask to be elevated through them?

Is your name Jacob or Israel?

-102

Wake up! Wake up! Don your strength, don the garments of your splendor. Shake the dust from yourself, arise, enthrone yourself, undo the straps on your neck.

Turn away! Turn away! Go forth from here. A contaminated person shall not touch you. Go forth from within. Cleanse yourselves, bearer of the vessels of G-d. Isaiah 52:1-52:11

These words were prophesied some 2,000 year ago.

Isaiah has given us the steps necessary to move from sleeping to awakening, for all times.

The word awake in Hebrew is Ohry, coming from Ohr, light.

First and foremost, the only force that can do the awakening is yourself. Don't wait for anything or anyone to put the garments of strength and splendor on you. Don't wait for circumstances to be a certain way, don't wait for people to be a certain way, don't wait for yourself to have achieved this and that in your mind.

Where ever you are at, whatever circumstance, whatever lack you feel you might have, you can, if you choose, put on the light, and put the garments of strength and splendor on yourself.

Second, shake off the dust. Shake off the years of accumulation of non-serving habits, thoughts, ideas, hang ups, walls, resistance, that has been compiled. Shake it off from yourself, now you awakened, now you have the light to see those thoughts, ideas within self that are not aligned with your highest and Divine self.

Shake it off.

Third, stand tall. When you have light, when you are aware, you become connected to your purpose. You are no longer walking in despondency wandering what to do, you have strength, light, and with that you stand tall.

You stand tall because of the light, and because of your awareness, not because someone gives you a medal, or that you are buoyed up by your surroundings.

You stand tall in going forth with knowingness, purpose, and awareness.

The standing tall here is not pride, but fortitude.

Once there is awareness, you can no longer be in same space.

One must turn away.

If there is hate, turn away

If there is doubt, turn away

If there is fear, turn away

If there is worry, turn away

If there is insult, turn away

If there is judgement, turn away

Everything is from within.

Awakening is from within.

Splendor and strength are from within.

Standing tall is from within.

Turning away is from within.

We are all bearers of vessel of G-d.

Dust can settle on us, chains of past can hold us hostage, slumber can come upon us. However, we can choose to don strength and splendor, by awakening.

Wake up!

Wake up!

Turn away!

Turn away!

You the bearer of G-d's vessel.

-103

*L*et love be your guiding light &
Let compassion be your internal compass.

Compassion is the ability to hold a space for other to be, whether in state of joy, or in state of pain. It's also the ability to give the warm, secure, protected space for the other to grow, expand and become.

Compassion shows itself in many different forms. One of the most powerful forms of compassion is listening and being fully present for the other.

Love is the ability to give to the other without a preconceived notion of why and how they deserve to be gifted with this energy, it wants nothing back, it's not based on need of self, rather the need of the other. It's the ability to be able to see the other beyond their own insecurities, fears, and doubts. At its purest form, it's the ability to get connected to someone's internal light without the facade of the others personality.

Loving someone gives them the ability to see themselves beyond their identities, beyond their weaknesses, and connect them to their own essence and internal light.

Love and compassion are transformative for the receiver as well as the giver.

Love creates possibilities.

One grows, develops, becomes, in a space of nurturance and nourishment.

Love allows the spark of creativity to be activated within the other, and gives them the confidence to step forth.

If these are all true for the other, how much more so for oneself.

Hillel says "love the other as you love yourself".

We can not give away something we don't have.

We can not be generous with an energy that sees beyond weakness, if we don't know what that is.

We can not hold a space for the other to grow and become, if we haven't been able to create that for ourselves.

Love is a force that's beyond time and space. To get connected to this force, first we must be able to open our own hearts, we must hold a space of compassion for our own selves, without the put downs, and harsh judgements.

Love is always always accompanied by forgiveness.

To be able to get connected to this force, we must be able to forgive ourselves, and not hold ourselves a hostage to our own severe judgements.

In this space we can grow, become, evolve.

Many times people think to love oneself is selfish. That's only if you'r getting connected to physical aspect of love.

I love myself, so let me go shopping.

I love myself, so let me do as I please.

That's not love, that's numbing our internal pain.

Love for self, comes in form of forgiveness, comes in form of connection to an inner light, comes in form of possibilities, comes in form of growth, awareness, and higher consciousness.

Are you able to forgive yourself?

Are you able to hold a space of compassion for yourself?

Are you able to get connected to the force of the universe?

Are you able to forgive the other?

Are you able to connect the other with their own light?

Are you able to hold a space of growth and nurturance for them?

Let your love be their guiding light

&

Let your compassion be their internal compass

-104

Today marks 40 days.

The intention for the 40 days was to bring about one degree of shift.

I pray that the intention has been served.

Together, we have been through so much.

From the start of these posts going back to February, we have been through the pandemic and everything that came with it, and most recently the riots and lootings.

Who would have thought?

Personally, my family has had a tragedy, loosing a great family member at a young age, my uncle, Daijan Benjamin Bolour.

Who would have known?

This group has given me the strength, Faith, trust, that I have needed to go through these times. Thank you!

It has given me the tangibility of being part of a greater whole, connected in ways that one wouldn't even fathom to understand, secured in knowingness that together not only we will get through it but grow through it. For me that has been a gift. Thank you!

On these posts, we have explored Jewish teachings, quantum physics, & lessons that H-Shem has embedded within nature.

Together, we have seen the power of words, the power of choice, the power of faith, the power of trust, the power of love, & the power of compassion.

We have explored the idols of our times, the superstitions that one must rid oneself of, and the shadows of self.

To step into our best selves, we must know that it's a process of a lifetime.

It doesn't happen overnight, nor is there a lightning that brings shift suddenly.

It's continuous awareness.

It's continuous shift from one reality to a soul vision reality.

It's definitely not easy, but definitely doable, and it's part of the reason for being here, to involve ourselves with the evolution of who we are.

These posts are based on my own thought processes. They are my own writings. They are the questions I ask myself.

All the posts for the 40 day journey, have been written around 5 am. They have been based on the thought or inspiration of that morning.

I am eternally grateful to all of you, for giving me an opportunity to be part of this magnificent group.

I am grateful that you have given me an opportunity to grow and shift with you.

I am grateful to have created a bond together that's beyond time and space.

Even though the 40 days of writing has come to a close, our journey of self-awareness, connection, elevation, and growth continues.

Going forth, I will not post on a regular basis.

I will be posting randomly as I am moved and inspired by a learning, teaching, and awareness. Please feel free to remove yourselves from the group at anytime that you feel it no longer serves your growth.

I dedicate the 40 days to my beloved uncle, Benjamin Bolour, who was the personification of kindness, and my beloved grandmother, Talat Bolour, whose yartzeit is tomorrow, 5th of Tammuz.

May it serve as an elevation for their soul.

The word represents an aspect of our soul, that if we choose, we can be cognizant to bring forth, and allow to shine through.

It serves as for us to remember that aspect within self and give it our own dimension within the context of our lives.

It is for us to unleash the power embedded with our soul as given access by the word, through our oen thoughts, speech and action.

Generosity

Buoyant

Reverence

Resilience

Equanimity

Luminescent

Perseverance

Humility

Courageous

Aspiration

Patience

Empathy

Willpower

Discernment

Boundless

Benevolent

Presence

Fortitude

Foresight

Balance

Serenity

Conduit

Sincere

Vivacious

Expansive

Cohesive

Gratitude

Heroic

Honest

Tenacious

Integrative

Jubilant

Evolve

Sacred

Magnanimous

Prolific

Dignity

Transcendence

Perpetual

Light

Incandescent

Tranquil

Versatile

Transparent

Receptive

Compassion

Integrity

Commitment

Limitless

Worthy

Self-discipline

Healthy boundaries

Flexible

Loyalty

Surrender

Transform

Forgive

Envision

Perception

Devotion

Earnest

Being of service

Intention

Purposeful communication

Cultivate

Inspire

Freedom of choice

Determined

Action

Shape-shifter

Conscientious

Respect

Iconoclast

Responsibility

Jubilation

Open-heart

Enthusiasm

342 — Farangiss Sedaghatpour

Divine expression

Supportive

Faith

Rooted in Faith — 345

Righteousness

Our mission in life is to become righteous, to become deeply rooted in our faith and trust in G-d while at the same time bearing fruits of our actions.

This is no small feat. It requires day to day awareness. It requires us to toil, sometimes struggle with what's in front of us.

It requires patience and great tenacity. Like a tree that withstands storms, hurricanes, seasonal changes, extreme cold, extreme hot, we too are to stand changes, while growing, both inward, and outward.

One of the ways of doing this, is to remind ourselves daily of the qualities embedded within our soul, and evoking them on a continuous basis.

Our soul is multi-faceted, dynamic, and inter-dimensional. However, it relies on our conscious effort to awaken its inherent qualities.

We are courageous, resilient, luminescent, humble, benevolent, generous.

We are all empathetic, compassionate, kind, and sincere. We are both conduit of light and its expression, tranquil and jubilant at the same time.

We are everything all at once, however, it awaits us to bring it to our daily life. It requires us to bring it to our daily life. It requires us with laser sharp focus to channel our energy into direction of inherent qualities.

Use the words in the context of your own life.

Use your own guidance system to come up with best analogy for the words to be used on daily basis.

The word love was never used.

Love is the expression of all these qualities. Love is all of them love is supportive, enthusiastic, respectful, has healthy boundaries, takes action, is responsible, is determined, and is always in service.

Love is what a righteous person represents.

A righteous person, patiently grows, with beautiful branches and fruits.

Under its shade people rest, unto its trunk, people take support from its fruit, people get nourished, and yet, it takes nothing away from it.

Be righteous, be love, be a deeply rooted tree.

Questions open up the space to explore, evolve, to become.

Sometimes, it's not even answering the question but rather just staying with the question and allow it to marinate in our psyche.

The greatest form of speech is the ability to ask question.

We start an internal jouney, one that hopefully will loosen our hold on things that hold us limited and free us to do what we are here to do, to be a channel for divine light and allow that light to permeate all of physical reality.

— What is the highest vision that you can hold for yourself?

— Where have I been giving away my life force and energy to unworthy causes?

― How does the darkness of the world distract me from seeing my Divine path?

⏤ How can I be a better example to those who are in my energy field?

▬ What do my words transmit to the world outside of me?

— Am I expressing my faith on a daily basis within the context of my circumstances?

‐ Am I willing to let go of criticizing others, life circumstances, and myself?

‐ Am I willing to discern the lessons learned from the perceived mistakes and make them into virtues?

― If I have to be liberated from something what would that be?

― Is it from attachments, outdated ideas, pain, hurt, unforgiveness, sadness, grudge, shame?

― Do I have the courage to look at which areas of my life I have not tapped into humility?

― Am I willing to use my humility as virtue in those areas in future?

— If I can make a leap into an elevated future, what am I willing to leave behind?

— Am I able to pass over everything that might be holding me back, hold Divine hand, and be lead to my highest destiny?

▬ Am I able to identify one habit that's not in alignment with best version of myself?

— Am I expressing my faith on a daily basis within the context of my circumstances?

— How can I make more of an effort to learn and grow at this time?

— The journey of a thousand miles begins with first step.

— What step can I take today to begin the journey of my dreams?

— Can I be consistent?

— If not, why do I stop myself from being consistent?

— Do I give up easily?

— Have I left pieces of myself in past experiences and with people whom I'm not at peace with?

— Am I willing to start redeeming parts of myself that's been left behind?

— What am I willing to do to accomplish that?

— Is forgiveness part of that process?

▬ Are there any areas of my life where I am stubborn?

▬ Is it possible to have more flexibility in those areas?

— If I could declutter my brain, what are some files that I can delete?

— What are some files that are outdated and no longer in use, but I'm holding on like a precious stone?

— By deleting these files, how much space can open up in my brain for joy and creativity?

— Where have I felt powerless in my life?

— Do I still feel powerless in similar situations?

— How am I able to build myself up so that I would not feel powerless if similar situations arise?

→ Have there been instances where I have given up my dignity for approval?

→ Do I continue to do for approval?

→ Am I willing to exchange approval for my dignity?

— Have I been in circumstances where I have felt the need to lie?

— If yes, what has been the payoff of those lies?

— Has it been to look good in front of others, to represent something that it's not, or to protect something or someone?

— Am I willing to hold honesty on high ground and to walk that path?

— How can my limitations be changed to gifts and virtues?

— Is it through my mindset?

— Is it through my approach?

— Is it through my breaking through?

— What is my greatest fear?

— Is it validated?

— Does it apply to today?

— Can I let it go?

⌒ How much of past events is occupying my space in the now?

⌒ Am I willing to say farewell to some events, memories, so space is opened up for what needs to come in?

▬ Are there deep places within that's carrying shame and guilt?

▬ How much of my choices is effected by that?

▬ Am I willing to learn from the experiences, letting it become wisdom, and at the same time release the shame and guilt?

– What is the chatter in my headspace throughout the day?

– Who am I talking with?

– Can part of the chatter be changed into intentional conversations within my own headspace that engages my soul?

— If I could give a percentage to my inner joy what would that be?

— 30%, 40%, 50%........?

— If I could increase that by 1%, what would I do differently today?

— What would I add to my daily activity?

— If I could bring my emotional state into alignment with my wellbeing, what needs to be refined?

— Can I recognize events in the past where Divine providence has openly took my hand and lead me to where I need to go?

— If so, can I trust that I will be lead in future to where I need to be?

— If so, can I let worries about future dissipate?

— Do I have the patience and capacity to hold the unknown while waiting for the known to reveal itself?

- When I enter a room, do I judge people right away?

- Do I judge them by what they look?

- Do I judge them by what they are wearing?

- Cen I become more aware of the judgements I make automatically?

- Can I refrain from categorizing people by what they look like, what they are wearing, and instead see them for the person they are?

- Can I give myself space of no judgement, till at least I have gotten to know them a bit better?

- Am I able to empathize with people who are going through a difficult situation?

- How do I express that empathy to them?

- Do I show up for them?

—Do I maintain my integrity through my interactions during the day?

— What seeds have I planted in the past, that I'm seeing the fruits of today?

— What seeds can I plant today that I can reap the benefits of in the future?

— How does my light effect others?

— How does my darkness effect others?

— Am I able to increase my light to dark ratio in increments?

— What would those increments look like?

— Which part of myself/my life do I identify myself with most?

— Am I all that?

— Can I be more than that identification?

— Is there room for growth?

— Is there room for expansion?

— Who do I look up to or admire?

— What are the qualities that I admire most abouth them?

— Can I see those qualities within myself, as hidden as it might be?

— Can I enhance those qualities within myself, as small as they might be?

➖ What's the distance between action of another person and my reaction?

➖ Can this distance be increased even if it's seconds?

— How does my inner fire manifest itself?

— Does it serve the greater good?

– What is my contribution to the world outside of myself?

– Is it all inclusive?

– Is it soley for the sake of contribution?

– If already doing so, is there more of me that has not yet been tapped into to contribute?

– Can I do more?

— Am I aware of the gifts forgiveness presents?

— Am I willing to spend the next week forgiving one person a day, as hurtful as the situation might have been or as inconsequential as the situation might have been?

— What would be the outcome if I stopped giving energy to that which is not in my best interest?

— How often do I tap into the well of inspiration that's our Divine gift?

— Am I able to bring that inspiration into physical reality?

➻ How often are my decisions aligned with my heart?

→ Within this season of life, what are the gifts that are presenting themselves?

→ What is wanting to be known?

→ What are the lessons?

— If I was able to look at a problem from a different lens, what would I see?

— How might that effect my decision making?

▬ Can I get the nurturance, love, confidence, approval, that I need, from H-shem, rather than outside sources?

▬ How might that change my decision making?

- Am I afraid of future?

- What about the future am I afraid of?

- Do I know for sure that which I am afraid of will materialize?

- Can I be present to today and do to my best ability, with knowledge and wisdom at hand?

- Can I entrust the future into the hands of All Knower, All Healer, and the ultimate Miracle worker---H-Shem?

- How will that change my inner dialogue and emotional makeup for the day?

- If I could press the refresh button, what outdated thoughts, ideas, habits, attachments, needs to be refreshed?

- Am I willing to refresh?

- If I am willing, what steps do I need to take in order to move into that refreshed paradigm?

- Do I like the presence of my own company?

- If yes, what do I enjoy most about spending time with self?

- If not, why don't I like my own company?

- How might I shift that?

- Do I get uncomfortable being by myself for a time longer than I'm used to?

- What makes me uncomfortable?

- Can I shift in ways that I am in good company at all times, with self?

- How might that shift my mood?

- How might that shift my perception?

— Where in my expression of love and compassion, am I holding back?

— Does forgiveness need to take place?

— What else is holding me back?

— In what ways may I more fully engage in my outward expression of kindness, love and compassion?

▬ Having the inner light of soul, how can I put this light back in the universe?

▬ How may I be of service?

⌐ I pray that the questions can open up space within to be more and stand in greater light.

www.ingramcontent.com/pod-product-compliance
Lightning Source LLC
Chambersburg PA
CBHW071949070526
44583CB00015B/1117